On the Nā Pali Coast

On the Nā Pali Coast

A GUIDE FOR HIKERS AND BOATERS

Kathy Valier

A Kolowalu Book
University of Hawaii Press • Honolulu

93 92 91 90 89 88   5 4 3 2 1

Library of Congress Cataloging-in-Publication Data

Valier, Kathy, 1953–
  On the Nā Pali coast.

  (A Kolowalu book)
  Bibliography: p.
  Includes index.
    1. Hiking—Hawaii—Na Pali Coast—Guide-books.
2. Boats and boating—Hawaii—Na Pali Coast—Guide-books.
3. Na Pali Coast (Hawaii)—Description and travel—
Guide-books.   I.   Title.
GV199.42.H32N38   1988   919.69   88–1166
ISBN 0–8248–1154–2

Epigraph page: Hawaiian chant from Handy
and Handy, *Native Planters in Old Hawaii:
Their Life, Lore, and Environment,* Bishop
Museum Press, Honolulu, 1972. Lois S. H.
Johnson journal entry dated 4 September
1837, Hawaiian Mission Children's Society
Library.

To my parents,
Marjorie and Louis,
each of whom
guided me to a
deep love and
understanding
of nature

Wild is the sea at Kalalau, the waves pile high over each other.
An endlessly murmuring sea is the sea of Miloliʻi,
The sprays of the sea struggle upward,
The sea that pounds on the faces of the water-worn rocks,
The sea that spreads itself over the faces of the stones.

Hawaiian chant translated by Mary Kawena Pukui

The *Palii* baffles all my powers of description. It indeed
surpasses all that I have ever seen in sublimity. It extends
along the shore of the ocean for many miles and it almost
seems as you sail along as if it[s] towering peaks which seem
to reach to heaven . . . would lose their balance and over-
whelm you beneath [their] ruins in the mighty deep. Here
might the painter find scope for the boldest touch of his
pencil and here the poet gather[s] laurels for his brow.

From the journal of Lois S. H. Johnson, 1837

CONTENTS

LIST OF MAPS

ACKNOWLEDGMENTS

These pages are filled with the contributions of numerous people, who I hope will smile upon finding their mark within.

Foremost my gratitude goes to my husband, Norman, because no tree can sprout and grow without rich, nourishing soil. Ev Wingert patiently answered my endless technical questions about maps, while his quiet confidence in the completion of this project spurred me on. Jane Eckelman's cheerful support and that of my cartography classmates were invaluable. The facilities at Manoa Mapworks enabled the completion of many of the maps.

My informal editors generously gave their precious time and lent their expertise to this work. The abundant suggestions and contributions of these people left me feeling more like an editor than an author: Majorie Valier, Audrey Newman, Peggy and Victor Pavel, Martha Yent, Bill Gorst, Francis and Hal Frazier, Dick Logan, Joel Davis, Dave Boynton, Tim Flynn, and Don Heacock. I am also indebted to Jean Brady, formal editor, for the clarity she gave this work and for her eye for detail.

A special *mahalo* to Roger Watson and John Brizdle, who as employers nurtured my interest in Hawaiiana and as friends encouraged my continued growth in that direction.

The Division of State Parks, Bishop Museum, Hawaiian Mission Children's Society Library, Kaua'i Historical Society, Pacific Tropical Botanical Gardens, and the Wilcox Collection at the Kaua'i Regional Library yielded many of the nuggets of information dispersed throughout this work.

USING THIS GUIDEBOOK

For curious explorers this book offers another view of the Nā Pali Coast—the ruins and forest serve as windows through which Hawai'i's vital past can once again be witnessed. The astounding beauty of Nā Pali still speaks its own eloquent language, where once a vigorous culture thrived on the bounty coaxed from the soil and harvested from the sea. Sweeping changes have silenced these valleys, and their inhabitants have evaporated into the mist of the past. Now only rock walls glimpsed through the encroaching forest and an array of tropical plants remain to testify to this culture.

This guide synthesizes information gained from years of exploring and gleaned from 100 pounds of books—enough to break the back of the hardiest hiker. It is a guide to the natural and cultural history of this coastline; it is not simply a hiking book. For information on trail conditions and camping, contact the Division of State Parks. A helpful list of items useful for hiking and camping, as well as general trail information are available from Hanalei Camping and Backpacking.

The northeast section of the Nā Pali Coast is accessible only by trail; the northwest section can be seen only by boat. To give a complete view of the coast this guide has been divided into two sections, both starting at the east end where the trail and most boat rides begin. Each section stands on its own yet complements the other. The trail guide gives detailed information to suit a hiker's pace, while the section for boaters gives a quick overview of the valleys along the trail, concentrating on the valleys accessible only by sea. Those who read both sections will find some overlap—at Kalalau Valley, for instance. Boaters might want to read the hiking section to learn more about the coast, or as an effortless armchair hike. Hikers can, likewise, "see" the remainder of the coastline that is inaccessible on foot.

As part of this journey into the past, Hawaiian words are used throughout the text as a means of sharing commonly used terms. In telling directions, for instance, we refer to a place as *mauka* (inland, or toward the mountains) or *makai* (toward the sea) rather than north and south. Often a Hawaiian name reveals some insight into the native way of life or way of thinking. The glossary defines basic Hawaiian words and includes the scientific names of plants and animals.

Westerners ignominiously draped the Hawaiian language with an alphabet that never quite fit right, so darts and tucks were added to help reveal the body hidden beneath the dowdy garment. Using only five vowels and seven consonants left unused yardage: b, c, d, f, g, j, q, r, s, v, x, z. Subtleties in pronunciation have thus been preserved using the macron (ˉ) and glottal stop ('). For example: *nu'alolo 'aina* is a meal of *nu'alolo; nu'alolo 'ainā* means a stiff, aching *nu'alolo; nu'alolo aina* would be a place for procreation, while the crackling sound ('a'ina) would make for a noisy *nu'alolo*. Nu'alolo 'Āina, then, is the place whose name describes the valley's land, or *'āina*. Similarly, something as simple as *ao* could be: *ao*, meaning "daylight"; *a'o*, meaning "doctrine"; *'ao*, meaning "a new leaf"; or *'a'o*, the Newell's shearwater, heard at Miloli'i.

Points of interest along the Kalalau Trail are numbered in the margin of the text and correspond to numbers on the detailed maps that accompany the hiking section. Some points also correspond to mileage stakes that were originally set up in the 1960s but are no longer maintained. Unmarked stakes are likewise located on the maps, but use of the map scale is advised to determine distances.

Maps in this guide are varied to best suit the individual needs of boaters and hikers: boaters need an ocean view to easily identify points of interest, while ridges and valleys along the trail stand out more clearly on aerial photos than on contour maps. Maps did not exist with enough detail to show the stops mentioned in the hiking section, but aerial photos do. For this reason many of these maps are not to exact scale, although they offer a good idea of general distances and relative locations.

Use the information in this guide responsibly. Do not attempt to retrace ancient Hawaiian trails; I mention these trails only for your interest—goats and weathering have erased the original paths and only deadly, crumbling cliffs remain. Do not eat anything unless you know what it is and have tried it before. Even edible plants can cause severe allergic reactions, and 9 hours away from help is no place to discover that you are fatally allergic to mango fruit. Heed the warnings set up by the state: purify water before drinking it, stay out of the surf, and use caution during heavy rains—the trail gets treacherous and streams can rise unexpectedly. Stay on established trails. Please also note that the state allows hunting along the Nā Pali Coast at various times and places throughout the year, see text for details.

Conditions along the coast are ephemeral and defy all generalizations. Doubtless you will find it wet where I indicate that it should be dry, or what should be in bloom will not be, so please read this rendering of the coast with an eye to the playful way of nature. I eagerly welcome your suggestions and comments.

NĀ PALI COAST STATE PARK

Nā Pali Coast State Park encompasses 6,500 acres of the northwestern coast of the island of Kaua'i. The spectacular terrain along this coastline plunges from an elevation of 4,000 feet to sea level over a distance of less than 2 miles. This 15-mile stretch of coastline has stymied road builders—it is one of the least-disturbed wildlands in Hawai'i. The isolation of the Nā Pali Coast valleys makes them unique in all of Hawai'i; the rocky crags along the coast still harbor the vestiges of Hawaiian civilization and protect rare species of plants found nowhere else in the world.

George Dixon, the first European explorer to sail along the Nā Pali Coast, wrote in 1789 in his book, *A Voyage Around the World,* that he ". . . could not see any level ground or the least sign of this part of the island being inhabited. . . ." Indeed, even today while traveling by boat it is difficult to see even the bright nylon tents of campers.

Contrary to Dixon's observation most of these valleys were inhabited. As early as A.D. 1200 Hawaiians began to settle the coastline—farming in the valleys and establishing fishing settlements along the beaches. The lack of census data for the period makes it impossible to tell how many natives lived in the area when the first *haole*s, or foreigners, arrived on Kaua'i. However, the remnants of agricultural terraces tell us that Hawaiians farmed all of the usable land along the coast.

The last Hawaiian family, or *'ohana,* moved out of the area in 1919. Today a wealth of temple platforms, agricultural terraces, and house sites give testament to the extensive historical habitation of the coastline.

FORMATION OF THE COASTLINE

The spectacular views of the Nā Pali Coast's rugged scenery make a vivid impression on visitors, yet when volcanic activity on Kaua'i's northwestern coastline ended 6 million years ago there were no cliffs on the coast at all. Instead, the entire island of Kauaʻi was dome-shaped and the coast extended in a gradual slope a mile farther out to sea than it does at present. If you had stood at the road's end at Kēʻē Beach 6 million years ago you would have found yourself under 1,000 feet of solid lava rock.

Ten million years of volcanic eruptions built the Hawaiian Islands to their greatest height, and Hawaiʻi's beaches now stand 3 miles above the seafloor. Volcanoes are still building the southern end of the island chain. How were deep valleys and knife ridges formed from these huge lava domes? The Nā Pali Coast is the result of a 6-million-year contest between solid lava rock and persistent erosion. Kauaʻi's thundering winter surf and torrential rain have etched their mark in the northwestern corner of the original shield volcano, laying bare the gridwork of the lava layers and dikes you see today. These forces continue to drive the land back into the sea. Hawaiians aptly named this piece of nature's handiwork *Nā Pali,* which means "the cliffs."

HAWAIIAN SETTLEMENT OF NĀ PALI

Settlement of Nā Pali was the final chapter in the saga of Polynesian migrations eastward across the Pacific, which began in the Malay Peninsula 1600 years before Christ. Archaeologists have found indications that Polynesian people from islands over 2,000 miles to the south arrived in Hawaiʻi more than 1,500 years ago.

From a tangle of mythology and fact comes the tales of the Mū and Menehune—people who inhabited Kauaʻi before the later migrations from the south. Pushed into the interior of the island by more-aggressive newcomers, these people soon vanished and their role in Hawaiian history was relegated to mythology.

The dating of materials from sites at Kēʻē Beach indicate that the north shore of Kauaʻi was inhabited by A.D. 1000. Over the centuries Hawaiʻi's burgeoning culture spread into the valleys along the coast, advancing to Nuʻalolo Kai by A.D. 1400—a time when plagues, bitter winters, and political decline ravaged medieval Europe.

Between the produce of farms flourishing in the lush tropical valleys and good fishing from the beaches and reefs, natives had all they needed to live comfortably. Gradually the Hawaiians pushed back the jungle, building rock walls to level off terraces for irrigated farming and to serve as platforms for their thatched huts. Years of back-wrenching labor went into fashioning these stone structures and the temple platforms that followed.

The Hawaiians along Nā Pali met their first Westerners in 1822 and 1837, when missionaries, who eventually established a small school and church in Kalalau Valley, first visited the coast. European ways, however, did not drastically change the lifestyle of the inhabitants of the coast as happened elsewhere in Hawai'i. Instead the rugged setting helped to insulate the native way of life until the early 1900s.

LATER LIFE ALONG THE COAST

Farming and fishing along the coast continued into the early twentieth century. In addition to the native food crops of taro, banana, and sweet potato, early *haole* settlers grew coffee in some of the valleys. Susceptibility to foreign diseases affected Hawaiians as it did the American Indians; epidemics swept through and decimated the native population. Many of the residents who survived the epidemics left their Nā Pali homes when the school at Kalalau closed. In 1847 Kalalau Valley had 190 residents, but by 1920 the people had left Nā Pali for the economic and social centers in Hanalei and Waimea.

Although during this century cattle grazed along Nā Pali, ranching lasted only from 1920 to the 1970s. The area then became part of the Territorial Forest Reserve. Although groups of adventurers or hunters occasionally visited the coast, its reputation of being inaccessible shrouded the area in an aura of mystery.

Disillusioned by man's inhumanity to man, Bernard Wheatley, a physician, made a pilgrimage to Kalalau. He stayed until the mid-1960s seeking peace of mind. A wave of newcomers flowed into Nā Pali in the late 1960s after Wheatley's departure. They settled into the valleys by the hundreds—plastic lean-tos sprang up where thatched huts once stood. Place names like "Big Pool," "Fat City," and "Bobo's Rock" replaced now-forgotten Hawaiian names. Visitors to Kalalau during this era recall its inhospitable residents, crowded conditions, and poor sanitation. These problems led the state government to make Kalalau a state park and limit the number of campers and their length of stay in the valleys. By 1984 the Nā Pali Coast State Park included three-quarters of the northwestern coast of the island.

A BRIEF NATURAL HISTORY

Except for one hermit and the vagabonds who moved through the area during the last two decades, permanent human habitation ended in the

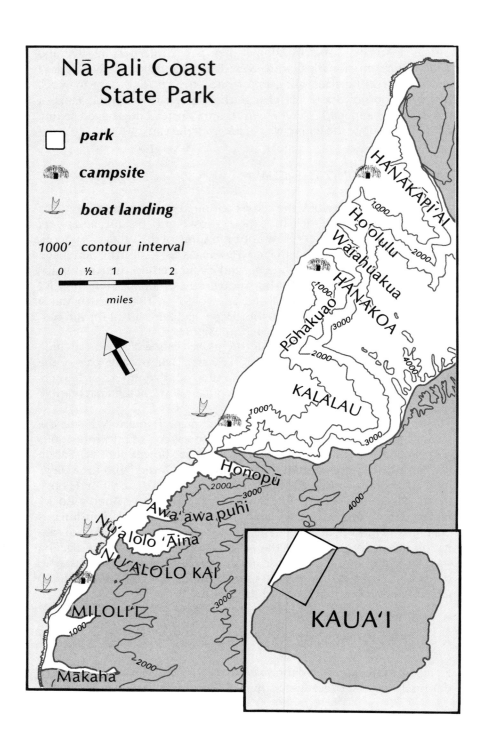

Nā Pali Coast State Park

☐ **park**

🛖 **campsite**

⚓ **boat landing**

1000′ contour interval

0   ½   1   2

miles

HANAKĀPĪ'AI

Ho'olulu

Waiahuakua

HANAKOA

Pōhakuao

KALALAU

Honopū

Awa'awapuhi

Nu'alolo 'Āina

NU'ALOLO KAI

MILOLI'I

Mākaha

KAUA'I

area in 1919. Now only the incised lava cliffs, an array of tropical plants, and the wildlife remain to fascinate visitors to the Nā Pali Coast.

Here botanists still find plants that grow only in Hawai'i, many of which have been wiped out in less-protected parts of the state. These endemic plants evolved from ancestors whose seeds occasionally landed here during the millions of years before man's arrival. Some plant varieties have become so specialized that they grow only in one valley and nowhere else in the world.

Many plants in Nā Pali Coast State Park found their way here without help from man, a remarkable feat considering that the Hawaiian Islands are the most remote place on Earth; no other scrap of high, volcanic land lies farther from any major island or continent. Imagine Kaua'i's 550 square miles floating in 68 million square miles of ocean. Somehow seeds blew here on the wind, floated on the sea, or hitchhiked on birds' feathers or in their guts: the process of reaching Hawai'i would be something akin to pitching poppy seeds at a postage stamp floating in a swimming pool.

Plants whose seeds made this incredible journey without the aid of man, and are common elsewhere in Polynesia, are called indigenous plants. *Naupaka,* a common beach shrub with jade green leaves, is one common indigenous plant; others include the *hala* and some varieties of *ko'oko'olau,* both of which you will meet along the trail.

The Hawaiians brought with them the plants necessary for food, clothing, medicines, and various handicrafts. Taro, banana, and sweet potato plants first came to Hawai'i on Polynesian voyaging canoes, carefully wrapped in moist moss and leaves and nurtured during the month-long journey.

Introduced plants from other tropical regions of the world also abound in these valleys. In the summer months the coastline becomes a cornucopia of edible fruit such as guava and passion fruit from Brazil and mango from India. Over the years these introduced plants have squeezed out the native plants. Hikers wearing shorts quickly become familiar with the thorny lantana bush, a rambunctious introduced ornamental plant that escaped into the wilds. Many areas are shaded by the foreign Java plum (not from Java and not a type of plum) with its olive-sized purple fruit.

Many visitors notice the lack of wild animals along the coast. Campers need not hide food from raccoons or bears. No squirrels bound from the trees nor, happily, does the presence of snakes necessitate carrying snake-bite kits. Goats are probably the most conspicuous residents of the valleys. Between December and April majestic humpback whales breach offshore during their winter vacation in Hawai'i's warm waters. Less obvious are the native stream creatures, like the *'o'opu,* a native fish, and *'ōpae,* a native shrimp. Two local lizards, the gecko and skink, scurry among the rocks. Graceful native seabirds and an international array of birds ply the skies, including the gray Brazilian cardinal with his jaunty red crest and the shama thrush from India, whose elegant repertoire of songs graces the forest.

The northeast tradewinds wrap around the north coast of Kaua'i providing a wide variation in rainfall. The luxuriant rain forest in Hanakāpī'ai gives way to an arid landscape at Miloli'i complete with prickly pear cacti. Winter brings increased rainfall and powerful ocean swells. The resulting surf eats away the sand beaches formed by summer's gentle currents, as Mother Nature rolls up her welcome mat to swimmers. After hiking miles to these beaches visitors are dismayed at finding only rocks with at best a token swatch of sand.

Scouring winter surf laden with sand prevents reefs from forming along much of the coast. Only at Kē'ē Beach, Miloli'i, and Nu'alolo Kai does coral growth support a rich community of marine life. Here fishing is usually good during the summer months—after the fish have had a winter respite from hungry fishermen.

VISITING THE NĀ PALI COAST

Even the Hawaiians had difficulty getting to various valleys along the Nā Pali Coast, so they built a network of trails to gain access to all parts of the coast when winter surf made boat travel too dangerous. Since the last natives left their Nā Pali homes the jungle and erosion have reclaimed all but the Kalalau Trail.

Today the majority of visitors see the coast as a fleeting view from a helicopter cabin, but actually to set foot in the park you must travel either by boat or on foot. Commercial boats with the proper landing permits stop at Kalalau Beach, Nu'alolo Kai, and Miloli'i Beach in the summer months. The 11-mile-long Kalalau Trail starts at Kē'ē Beach on Kaua'i's north shore and winds through four valleys before reaching its destination, Kalalau Valley.

Although day-trips down the coast are easier to arrange, overnight stays offer greater rewards for those willing to take the time. In the summer the sun sets in the sea, offering visitors a chance to see the illusive green flash—a splash of green light that occurs at the exact moment the sun sinks below the horizon. Far from city lights you can catch a majestic view of our galaxy—the Milky Way—and the constellations. Camping is allowed at Hanakāpīʻai, Hanakoa, Kalalau, and Milo-liʻi. Camping permits are required and there are restrictions on length of stay at each campground. Permits must be picked up in person from the Division of State Parks; some form of identification is required before a permit can be issued.

HIKING THE KALALAU TRAIL

THE TRAILHEAD AT KĒʻĒ BEACH

Driving north on Highway 560 you come to the road's end 40 miles from Līhuʻe town. Here at Kēʻē Beach the Kalalau Trail begins on the *mauka* (toward the mountain) side of the road. The tranquil trailhead at Kēʻē Beach belies its vibrant heritage. Hawaiian legends tell us that the handsome chief Lohiʻau danced here before the spirit form of the fiery goddess Pele, inciting the passion that gave this area its name, Hāʻena, meaning "the heat." A similar name, Kaʻena, which also means "the heat," was given to hot, dry places on Oʻahu and Lānaʻi.

Today you can touch the past by visiting the hula platform where Lohiʻau once danced. To locate the platform walk out on the *mauka* side of Kēʻē Beach, skirting just above the boulder beach. The house that you pass on the point belonged to architect John Allerton until his death in 1986, at which time it was taken over by the state. The house previously belonged to John's adopted father, Robert, a wealthy landscape designer from Illinois, who moved to Kauaʻi in 1937. On Kauaʻi, the Allertons are best known for their beautiful estate in Lawai Kai near Spouting Horn. Tours of that estate can be arranged through the Pacific Tropical Botanical Gardens.

Continue past the house and walk uphill until you come to the large stone foundation of a *heiau,* or Hawaiian place of worship. Above, the remains of the *hālau hula* where Lohiʻau once danced stand at the base of the cliff. This humble-looking rock platform was the most important *hālau hula* in all of Hawaiʻi. Young men and women came here for months of rigorous training in a strict religious atmosphere to learn dances that recounted legends and invoked favors from the gods.

Try to imagine how this *hālau hula* platform once looked: imposing carved images surrounded three thatched huts, one of which housed an altar dedicated to Laka, Hawaiian deity of the hula. Following the death of Kamehameha the Great in 1819, his successor, Liholiho (Kamehameha II), ordered the destruction of all *heiau* buildings, altars, and carvings, so that today only the rock platforms remain.

Lohi'au's
house
Kalalau
Trail
houses
hālau hula
Hwy 560
heiau
0   200'
KĒ'Ē BEACH

3000
3000
2000
1000
HANAKĀPI'AI
1000
1000
2000
3000
1000
2000
HO'OLULU
WAIAHUAKUA

1
2
3
4
5

Hanakāpi'ai Beach

Kē'ē Beach

THE KALALAU TRAIL

0   ¼   ½   1
mile

KALALAU

HANAKOA

PŌHAKUAO

Kalalau Beach

Kalalau Trail

mileages

contour interval   200 feet

A final ceremony concluded the hula training, allowing the students to dance in public. At midnight before this graduation a solemn procession of nude initiates went to the sea for a symbolic cleansing. Offerings to Laka were then made and the altar bedecked with leis before the concluding feast.

On special occasions students of the hula still use this *hālau hula* platform, now property of the county of Kaua‘i.

On the boulder beach below the *hālau hula* stands a large rock where mothers brought their newborns' umbilical cords—the symbolic connection with the spirits of the child's ancestors—and wedged them into the rock's cracks. The rock was named after a lizard-like goddess, Kilioe. The Hawaiians considered it an ill omen if a rat stole the cord, believing that the child would grow up to become a thief.

A short walk *makai* (toward the sea) along Kē‘ē Beach will reward you with a first dramatic glimpse of the Nā Pali Coast. From the parking lot, head out to your right along the beach 100 yards or so until you can turn around and see the cliffs. The farther you walk, the better the view, but use caution in winter months when high surf makes this walk dangerous. You can see as far as Alapi‘i Point at Nu‘alolo Kai, 10 miles away. The intermediate point that looks like a rhinoceros' head lies on the far side of Hanakoa Valley, halfway to Kalalau Beach.

#1   As you approach the trailhead you will have a clear view through the trees of Makana Cliffs, which tower 1,500 feet above you. During special celebrations nimble Hawaiians scrambled up these cliffs to push burning branches off the top, leading to the nickname "Fireworks Cliff."

The trees shading the parking area include the ironwood with its fragile, needle-like leaves; the Java plum; and the tropical almond, with its large, oblong leaves. I have heard people 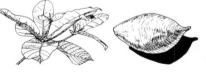 speculate that if you were stranded on a desert island with an endless supply of edible tropical almond nuts you would still starve, because getting into the nut uses up more calories than are supplied by it. Try breaking one open and see if you agree.

The ironwood, or casuarina as the Australians call their native tree, was introduced to Hawai‘i for planting as windbreaks. Although not a true pine tree, its slender, needle-like leaves have earned it the nickname "Australian pine." One of the problems with having plants from so many regions of the world is that they each have different names in every corner of the tropics. Thus our ironwood tree is also called casuarina, she oak, beefwood, and Australian pine.

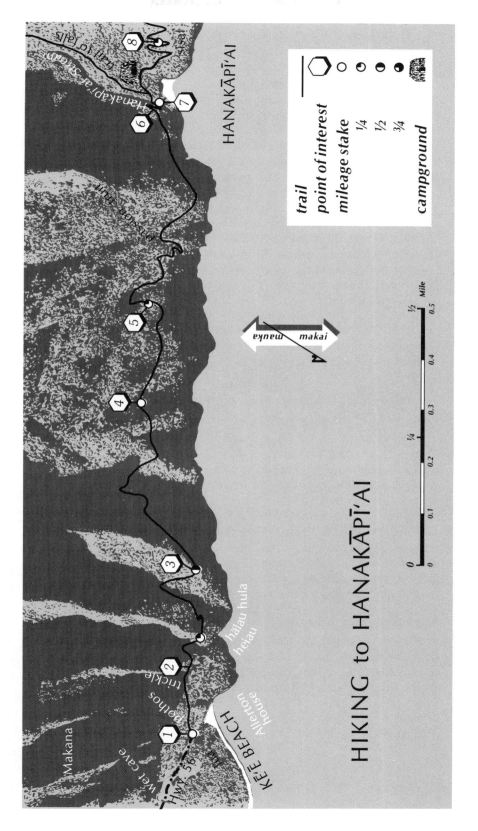

HIKING to HANAKĀPĪʻAI

Legend:
- trail
- point of interest
- mileage stake: ¼ ½ ¾
- campground

Scale: 0 — 0.1 — 0.2 — ¼ 0.3 — 0.4 — ½ 0.5 Mile

mauka ← → makai

HANAKĀPĪʻAI

Makana
Wet cave
Hwy. 56
pā
Allerton house
KĒʻĒ BEACH
pōhos
trickle
hālau hula
heiau
Joseph trail
Hanakāpīʻai Stream
Hanakāpīʻai Falls
Trail to Falls
salt

Java plum trees, with their 5-inch-long, shiny green leaves and blotchy bark, come from India where the astringent purple fruit is used in winemaking. The Hawaiians adapted the fruit as a basis for cloth dye. The fruit, which ripens in the fall, is edible and is good for jams and jellies, but visitors from the mainland find that its astringent  qualities remind them of chokecherries. When in bloom the Java plum sports pale yellow tufts—characteristic of the myrtle family to which it belongs. You will encounter many of its relatives along the trail, including 'ōhi'a, guava, and 'ōhi'a 'ai.

Keep an eye out for a cocky brown bird, about 9 inches tall, strutting around the parking area. A yellow blaze around its eyes makes the myna bird (a) easy to identify. Brought here in 1865, these scrappy birds with their ungainly gait and raucous squawk are the bullies of

(a)   (b)   (c)

Hawai'i's bird world. Brazilian cardinals (b) also frequent the road's end; their shock of red feathers contrasts with their conservative grey plumage. They share the skies with the familiar all-red cardinal (c), and both were introduced to Hawai'i in the 1920s.

None of Hawai'i's beleaguered native forest birds, such as the rare crimson and green-hued honeycreepers, live along the coast. Just as the Hawaiians fell victim to *haole* diseases, the native forest birds died from diseases introduced with foreign birds, like the myna. On Kaua'i only the highest mountains harbor native birds; above 4,000 feet there are no disease-carrying mosquitoes. Luckily, Kaua'i escaped the introduction of the mongoose, which eats birds' eggs.

Before you begin the trail take note of the rock wall hidden in the undergrowth to your left as you pass the trailhead sign. One of the first archaeologists to survey the area described this rock structure as the house site of Lohi'au. Hawaiians built the wooden frames for their thatched huts on rock-faced platforms like this one. Today, little remains to tell of the original structure except for the rock walls and platforms.

THE TRAIL

The Kalalau Trail was improved sometime in the late 1800s and extends 11 miles from the trailhead at Kē'ē Beach to Kalalau Valley. Much of the stone paving along the first mile of trail was laid when the trail was improved during the 1930s. The trail climbs and descends numerous times, making these 11 miles particularly arduous. After it leaves the Kē'ē Beach trailhead, only once, at Hanakāpī'ai, does the trail return to sea level. The highest elevation—800 feet—is reached near the trail's 3-mile mark.

Hanakāpī'ai, 2 miles in, is the first valley along the trail. Here you find a sand beach in the summer that erodes to a boulder beach in the winter. Hikers also enjoy the valley's freshwater stream and the additional 2-mile hike up the valley to a secluded waterfall.

Halfway to Kalalau the trail crosses Hanakoa Valley. The campsites at Hanakoa lie farther inland than those at Hanakāpī'ai. Most backpackers use Hanakoa as a layover stop on their way into Kalalau. You can reach a waterfall very similar to the one at Hanakāpī'ai by walking less than 1 mile *mauka* of the campsites.

Kalalau Valley is the largest valley on the coast and is known for its extensive archaeologial sites, waterfalls and pools, wild fruit, and excellent camping. The beach here marks the end of the trail, beyond which the cliffs make foot travel impossible.

HIKING TO HANAKĀPĪ'AI

The 2-mile hike into Hanakāpī'ai takes from 1 to 2 hours depending on how many stops are made along the way. Reports indicate that Hawaiians made this trip in 20 minutes.

The trail climbs steadily for the first mile, gaining over 400 feet in elevation—a grade that often discourages less-ambitious hikers. Persistence, however, is rewarded by a refreshing spring that marks the point halfway to Hanakāpī'ai. From here the trail descends to sea level over the next mile.

Even casual visitors are encouraged to walk the first ½ mile of the trail, as it offers a sweeping vista along the coastline and an aerial view of the coral reef off Kē'ē Beach. An opulent growth of pothos vines, some entwined around the trees, flanks the begining of the trail. These vines, related to the taro plant and the red, heart-shaped anthurium, have escaped from nearby gardens.

Beside the trail every ¼ mile you will see rusty metal stakes installed in the 1960s by the Hawaii State Division of Forestry. The state no longer maintains these trail markers, and their number decreases past Hanakoa Valley. Make a mental note of these markers as you pass them to help you locate points of interest mentioned in this book.

#2   The trail starts around the first ridge, past a small trickle of water that is used to supply the Allerton house. From the edge of the ridge you can look down and see the *hālau hula* and *heiau* next to the house.

Along this opening stretch of trail you will find an amazing yet unassuming plant, the *akoko*. The name refers to a group of plants that originated from one or two common ancestors and evolved into everything from ground covers to trees standing 25 feet tall. The seeds of coastal *akoko* floated to Hawai'i's beaches, while lowland varieties came by air. New plants arrived in these islands at the rate of only 1 every 70,000 years or so, allowing each newcomer plenty of time 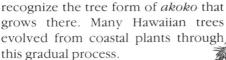 to adapt. As subsequent generations of *akoko* crept inland over thousands of years their form changed. Moving farther from the harsh, salty beach environment into the wet, nurturing interior of the islands, this ground-hugging plant evolved into a bush and eventually a tree. Although the plant form has changed, the leaves remain so similar among the various forms that after locating the *akoko* in this area you could go hiking in the mountains at Kōke'e in the Waimea district and recognize the tree form of *akoko* that grows there. Many Hawaiian trees evolved from coastal plants through this gradual process.

Notice those long, tan leaves littering the trail? They have fallen from *hala* trees above you. *Hala* is easy to identify by its complex supportive root structure. Known elsewhere in the world as pandanus, *hala* seeds floated here on ocean currents. When the seed casings dry out they resemble miniature brushes, hence Polynesians found them useful for painting designs onto their *tapa* cloth. In addition, the Hawaiians plaited leaves *(lau)* from the *hala* into mats, baskets, and even sails for their canoes: the leaves were stripped of their sawlike

edges before being soaked in salt water then cut lengthwise to a spe-
cific width. At present you will find *lau hala* crafts for sale in giftshops
on Kaua'i and elsewhere in the islands.

The ½-mile point, two ridges farther west along the trail, offers a   #3
dramatic view of the coastline. You can easily see the effects of the var-
iability in the pattern of rainfall as you look past the green cliffs flank-
ing Hanakāpī'ai to the red ridges between Honopū and Nu'alolo 'Āina.
At your present location 75 inches of rain fall annually, yet only 10
miles away at Miloli'i less than 20 inches fall each year. Boats often
leave Hanalei in the rain and arrive at Miloli'i to find it dry. I have
camped at Miloli'i and experienced only a light drizzle while flash
floods raged elsewhere on the island. The northeast tradewinds blowing up against the northeast side of Kaua'i force clouds to form and
relinquish their rain, so by the time this air has blown across to the
northwestern Nā Pali valleys it has little moisture left, leaving the
southwestern portion of the coast in a rainshadow.

The strong winds that usually buffet the ½-mile point are drawn
toward the arid western side of Kaua'i. If you drive past Kekaha town
on Kaua'i's west side you see this flat, dry area. On a typical summer's
day the plains around the Barking Sands area heat up. The hot air then
rises, sucking air from the north and south shores of Kaua'i as a
replacement; thus quiet mornings turn into windy afternoons. Boaters
pushing up the coast into the afternoon wind are especially aware of
this Jekyll-and-Hyde change in the coast's personality.

The islands of Lehua and Ni'ihau are visible from the ½-mile point.
Lehua rises 710 feet above the ocean and en-
compasses a total of 290 acres. No one lives on
the island, which is named after the *'ōhi'a
lehua* blossom. Early Hawaiians decorated hula
altars with these blossoms, the favorite flower
of Pele, the volcano goddess. She will cause it
to rain if you should pick these flowers. *'Ōhi'a*
trees cover the slope just before the ½-mile

point. When they bloom in March, the bright red tufts—the *lehua*
blossoms—are easy to spot. In the 1800s, ships carried dense *'ōhi'a*
wood to California to use as railroad ties.

To the left (south) of the island of Lehua the white sand beaches of
Ni'ihau are barely visible. The smallest inhabited island in Hawaii, it
measures only 18 by 6 miles. The beaches you see yield tiny, delicate
shells that, strung into exquisite leis, can sell for thousands of dollars.

The island of Ni'ihau is privately owned by a local *haole* family. The
island was purchased by the family for ten thousand dollars from

Kamehameha V in 1864. A great deal of mystique surrounds this dry island because its owners, the Robinsons, prize their privacy. Ranching is the main occupation for the residents of Ni'ihau, of which there are approximately 250. Although inaccurate rumors abound that claim all of Ni'ihau's inhabitants are full-blooded Hawaiians, it is the sole island in Hawai'i where only Hawaiian is spoken. Until the middle of this century the Robinson's Makaweli Ranch grazed cattle on the Nā Pali Coast as well.

Beyond the ½-mile point you find another native plant. Its Hawaiian name, *ko'oko'olau,* refers to some sixty native varieties of a plant that Hawaiians used for making tea. The seeds of introduced varieties of this plant, known as Spanish needle, will stick to your cuffs if you walk off the trail wearing long pants. Likewise, the two prongs on these needle-like seeds can cling to birds' wings, which is how the first seeds came to Hawai'i. After the original *ko'oko'olau* plants arrived here, however, the prongs gradually shortened and the needles changed shape. This adaptive process is typical of Hawaiian plants and birds, which, after their journey here, no longer need to maintain their means of travel. Without their prongs, the seeds of the native *ko'oko'olau* can no longer hitchhike, so those found on hiker's clothing must be from the introduced plant, Spanish needle.

Researchers from the Smithsonian Institution recently discovered bones of Hawaiian birds that through evolutionary changes had lost their ability to fly. Once settled in Hawai'i, where no predators threatened them, they evolved into flightless birds like the ostrich. Hungry Hawaiians finished off most of these birds before the first *haole* arrived.

Look for a relative of *ko'oko'olau,* known also as *oi* or Jamaica vervain, that bears boastful blue flowers on vertical spikes. This trailside weed is about 2 feet tall and has mintlike leaves that resemble *ko'oko'olau*. Natives in Central America used *oi* for medicinal purposes.

#4   By the 1-mile mark you will have climbed 400 feet to the highest point between Kē'ē Beach and Hanakāpī'ai. From this point the trail begins its drop into Hanakāpī'ai. Here two refreshing springs offer a cool excuse to stop and rest. These springs run throughout the year and reveal something about the complex geology hidden beneath the dense tropical vegetation. Farther down the coast barren ridges have been eroded, exposing a network of dikes that threads its way through the layers of lava rock. Dikes, vertical partitions of dense rock, separate porous lava flows. As rainfall seeps down through the sponge-like, porous lava, it reaches horizontal layers of dense rock, or sills. A series of dikes will hold water much like the walls of a water tank do. Along the Nā Pali Coast, springs occur wherever erosion eats into the sides of one of these natural water tanks, releasing its water.

Local hikers anchor glossy *ti* leaves in the spring's flow, which then arcs out in natural water fountains. The Hawaiians used *ti* leaves to wrap their food before cooking it in an underground oven, or *imu. Ti* leaves were also used to make skirts for the hula, and *ti* plants were grown around Hawaiian homes to keep away evil spirits.

The *'awapuhi*—a type of wild ginger—also grows in this area; rainwater caught in its up-turned flower cluster takes on the flower's spicy fragrance, making a natural shampoo. Green *'awapuhi* leaves sprout up in the spring; flowers pop up on separate stalks in summer; then the plant dies back in late fall.

Across the trail you will find banana plants, called *mai'a* by the Hawaiians. Technically a large herb, the banana plant produces fruit once and then dies, leaving new shoots around its base. Very few types of bananas produce seeds and those seeds are too heavy to reach Hawai'i on their own. Thus we deduce that Polynesian settlers brought bananas as one of their food plants.

According to the religious practices of early Hawaiians, women were allowed to eat only two of some fifty varieties of *mai'a* that grew in Hawaii. Their eating restrictions included other foods as well, so that men did the cooking and ate separately from the women. This *kapu* (taboo) arose from the belief that women were unclean because of their monthly menses.

Polynesians regarded *mai'a* as one of the forms taken by their god, Kanaloa. The mythical Mū people, who lived in the forests near Nā Pali, lived on *mai'a*. Unlike the legendary Menehune, Mū were not dwarf-like in size. The local term for hors d'oeuvre, *pūpū,* came from the Hawaiian practice of eating small, sweet bananas called *pūpū* after drinking the bitter narcotic *'awa.*

Farther along the trail about ¼ mile you will come to the top of a west-facing slope covered with *uluhe,* or false staghorn fern. This native fern dominates areas that have been stripped of vegetation. To the innocent eye this fern-covered slope looks like the epitome of tropical vegetation.

I grew up in Hawai'i assuming that the plants around me and the way they grew were the same as when the Hawaiians lived here, but I have since learned the truth. Many of the first captains who stopped in Hawai'i to resupply and refit their ships brought gifts for their Hawaiian hosts. In 1778 Captain Cook brought the first goats to Hawai'i and left them on Ni'i-hau thinking they could be bred to aug-ment the native pigs and dogs as a  source of meat. Two chiefs arguing over the goats killed them, but more goats arrived on the ships of Captain Vancouver, who brought cattle as well.

The Hawaiians allowed the cattle to run free, and the animals were protected by a *kapu* that forbade hunting them for the first ten years. This *kapu* was so successful that the last cattle were not finally elimi-nated from Kaua'i's forests until 1916. Meanwhile, goats and cattle chewed their way through the native forest. Plants had no need to pro-tect themselves with thorns or poisonous leaves because there were no grazing animals prior to the gifts of cattle and goats from the British seafarers.

All of the islands bear the scars of the destruction caused by over-grazing. Along the wetter section of the Nā Pali Coast, plants regener-ate quickly enough to keep up with the destruction. As you travel down the coast to drier areas, however, erosional scars become more noticeable.

Although the *uluhe* on this slope is a native plant, introduced plants generally invade disturbed areas and the arrival of weeds during the period of uncontrolled grazing only compounded the problem. Where native plants had been eaten away, seeds of hardy introduced plants sprouted up. Often birds spread these seeds in their droppings after eating foreign fruit, such as guava and *koa haole,* and few places escaped this aerial replanting process. Around 5,000 species of intro-duced plants have moved in to compete with 2,200 native varieties.

After traversing this slope you cross a small stream, then descend through a series of switchbacks. Past the 1½-mile mark two brooks have carved a small valley. Before crossing the second stream the trail passes under a natural arbor of passion fruit, whose flowers hang like fragrant blue chandeliers. Other varieties of passion fruit also grow in the park.

The trail eventually swings out around the ridge that forms the eastern side of Hanakāpīʻai, offering your first view of Hanakāpīʻai Beach, framed by *hala* trees. Owing to seasonal changes in the ocean's currents, in the winter only boulders make up this beach, but in late summer a glistening white sand beach forms.

Archers hunt for goats between this ridge and the far side of Hanakoa Valley. Be alert as there is no safety area along this segment of the trail, except around the Hanakāpīʻai and Hanakoa campsites. The state issues two-day permits for bow and arrow hunting throughout the year; up to fifteen people might be hunting here at any one time.

Soon vistas of Hanakāpīʻai Valley open before you. Across the valley mouth you can clearly see the trail switchbacks climbing up the west side of the valley and on to Hanakoa Valley. You might make out one or more waterfalls inland, depending on the amount of recent rainfall. The falls can be reached via a 2-mile-long trail that branches off the Kalalau Trail in Hanakāpīʻai Valley.

#6

A yellow-and-black striped concrete cylinder located one switchback above the valley floor marks the tidal wave, or tsunami, safety zone. Most visitors find it amazing that tsunamis can reach these elevations, yet during the 1957 tsunami startled residents in nearby Wainiha Valley watched the water reach the top of the utility poles located 100 yards inland.

Giant waves associated with the occurrence of earthquakes travel through the open ocean at speeds approaching 500 miles per hour. Bays shaped like those along Kauaʻi's north shore funnel these waves as they rush landward, forcing the water to expand upward. The resulting walls of water cause tremendous damage along Hawaiʻi's shorelines. About every 15 to 20 years large tsunamis associated with an earthquake occur in the Pacific Basin. When a tsunami wave threatens the Nā Pali Coast, Civil Defense notifies visitors of the danger via aircraft. Once above the markers, hikers are safe from danger.

Hanakāpīʻai Valley

Hanakāpīʻai literally means "bay sprinkling food." A myth also describes how a Menehune chiefess named Hanakāpīʻai died after giving birth. If you doubt the existence of Menehune, consider that in 1825 a census taker listed 65 of the 2,000 residents of nearby Wainiha Valley as Menehune.

Hawaiian place names, like Hanakāpīʻai, often have several possible interpretations, making them tricky to translate. Until Westerners brought the written word to Hawaiʻi, Hawaiians chose individuals to memorize their history, geneologies, and even their tax maps. Sadly, when writing was first introduced no one systematically wrote down all of this knowledge and gradually a huge segment of Hawaiian culture faded as these walking history books passed on. The meaning of many place names is thus no longer clear.

Hanakāpīʻai was the first valley along the coast to be settled by Hawaiians. They built their thatched *hale,* or houses, throughout the valley and along the beach, growing taro root, their staple starch, in flooded rock terraces. Other food crops such as banana, sweet potato, and arrowroot grew between the taro paddies. No census records exist to tell how many Hawaiians once lived in this valley.

Western civilization brought with it the caffeine habit. In 1899 W. E. H. Deverill of Hanalei planted 20,000 coffee trees in Hanakāpīʻai Valley, and maintained a house nearby that he and his family used on occasion. In the late 1800s a coffee mill was operated farther inland. The valley's economy also included taro, which was grown for export as recently as 1903. If you have time, take the branch off the Kalalau Trail that leads into the valley and see the rock remains of the Hawaiian settlement.

Hanakāpīʻai Stream

Continuing toward Hanakāpīʻai Beach you will cross Hanakāpīʻai Stream. If high water prevents you from crossing, the shore on the near side of the stream offers a good site for picnics. In periods of heavy rainfall this stream rises quickly, so think twice about crossing lest you get trapped on the far side or swept out to sea. The streams along this coast carry runoff water from relatively small areas, which means that high water will drop almost as quickly as it rises. Do not consider crossing a swollen stream—patience pays off better than a risky crossing.

While crossing Hanakāpīʻai Stream look for native stream animals darting out from under your feet. Five species of native freshwater

Taro growing in Hanakāpīʻai Valley, circa 1890. (From Bishop Museum photo collection)

fish, called *ʻoʻopu,* and a shrimp, called *ʻōpae,* abound in this stream. On a calm day I have watched the *ʻoʻopu* sunning themselves on the stream bed; put on a face mask, if you brought one, and take a look. These well-camouflaged fish, with a mottled black pattern on their backs, blend into the boulders. Four species of *ʻoʻopu* have suction cups on their stomachs—formed by the fusing of two fins—that allow them to latch securely onto rocks while the current flows past. These  fascinating fish, equipped with their suction-cup stomachs, can climb waterfalls. You probably know that salmon migrate from streams to the ocean to mature. An *ʻoʻopu* does the opposite; although they reproduce in streams, immature *ʻoʻopu* wash downstream to the sea to spend a few months before returning to the stream to complete their growth. The large sucker on the abdomen of the *ʻoʻopu* enables it to return to its stream home even if it means climbing waterfalls.

Like the *'o'opu, 'ōpae* spend part of their life cycle in the sea. Natives collected *'ōpae* by walking upstream with scoop nets slung between two scissorlike handles. Shaking these nets under rocks and plants along the stream dislodges the *'ōpae,* which then fall into the net.

Two less-visible inhabitants of these rivers are the Tahitian prawn and a mollusk, the *hīhīwai,* which the Hawaiians consider a great delicacy. *Hīhīwai* latch  on to the underside of boulders, from which natives would pluck them by hand. Tahitian prawns, introduced for eating purposes, have in turn become predators themselves and have destroyed much of the native stream life.

Competition with both hungry people and introduced animals takes its toll on Hawai'i's unique stream life. Like our plants, most species of *'o'opu* and *'ōpae* are endemic, and the scientists who study them hope to protect those threatened with extinction.

You might not be the only two-legged creature tottering across the streambed. Every winter a visitor from Alaska, the *'ulili,* or wandering tattler, flies to Hawai'i where it spends its days looking for edible invertebrates, such as small crabs, along the shores  and streams. This foot-long bird in its subdued gray plumage reminds me of a kindly old gentleman relentlessly searching for his spectacles.

After crossing the river, bear left and head uphill past the *lua,* or pit toilet. To proceed on to Hanakoa follow the trail that leads up the west valley wall.

Hanakāpī'ai Beach

Visitors to Hanakāpī'ai in the summer find an idyllic white sand beach; in the winter, however, the boulder rubble that greets hikers could hardly be called a beach. The digging action of the powerful winter surf scoops out sand, and ocean currents transport the sand out to sea where it is stored until the gentle summer surf pushes it back into place on the beach. Because of the relatively large number of visitors hiking to Hanakāpī'ai to use the beach, the state does not allow boat landings there.

Warning: Dangerous currents run along the coast throughout the year, so heed the signs. Even in the summer when the swells look small, a healthy, wind-driven current rips along the beaches, making swimming risky. Do not add another tragedy to the long list of drownings along the coastline. With the cool stream as a refreshing alternative you need not risk a swim in the sea.

In summer the beach sometimes extends to a U-shaped cave to the east (to your right as you face *makai*), which you can walk through. Just sitting in the shade of the *hala* trees, watching the endless procession of waves, can be enchanting. Doubtless Hawaiians spent their days in a similar fashion, as they plaited *lau hala* mats and baskets.

Behind the beach you will see a bush with bright green succulent leaves; snorkelers often crush these *naupaka* leaves and rub them inside their face mask to prevent condensation from forming.

The tiny (½-inch wide) whitish flowers of the *naupaka* bush (a) inspired numerous legends because they appear to be torn in half. One such legend involves a Hawaiian maiden of royal blood and a commoner who fell in love. Forbidden by law to see each other, they persisted until the *kahuna,* or priest, put the lovers to death as an example to all. As their souls departed the gods decided to honor them, making each into a *naupaka* plant. One type grows only in the mountains, while the other that you see here grows only by the sea; thus separating them as the law dictated. This explains why each plant, broken-hearted, produces only half of a flower.

(a)

Naupaka arrived before the Polynesians, thanks to its buoyant white seeds. The succulent, hairy leaves of this shrub store water, allowing *naupaka* to thrive along even the driest shorelines in Hawai'i.

The climb out of Hanakāpī'ai is less formidable than it looks, thanks to fourteen well-graded switch-backs. Partway up these switchbacks you pass the 2¼ mile marker; at this point look back to Kē'ē Beach where you started. Note the wave-cut terrace that forms a shelf below the cliffs along the coast. This bench is cut by the surging winter surf and by the debris the surf hurls against the cliffs.

#8

(b)

Sisal (b), a plant with huge, pointed leaves, abounds near the 2¼ mile marker. The name sisal probably sounds familiar—it was used extensively for making rope before synthetic materials became more popular. *Haoles* introduced sisal to Hawai'i in 1893 in an attempt to start a rope-making industry. Like its more familiar cousin, the century plant, sisal blooms about every ten years, putting up a stalk that looks like a 20-foot-tall asparagus. Tiny new sisal plants form on these tall stalks—safe from being eaten or trampled. There they dangle until the wind shakes them loose and they rain down by the hundreds, taking root wherever they fall. The protection of sisal's aerial nurseries explains the abundance of the plant along the coast.

Hanakāpī'ai Valley to the Falls

The trail to Hanakāpī'ai Falls begins on the west side of the stream and meanders up through several campsites under a canopy of guava. Camping is allowed here for one night only and requires a permit. Most campers use this site simply as a stopover on the way to or from Kala-  lau Valley. The guava trees you see in this area produce an egg-size fruit throughout much of the year. This edible fruit has a soft yellow skin and pink pulp. Since the introduction of guava from tropical America locals have used the fruit for making juices and preserves, and for flavoring baked goods. Kids on summer vacation make decent pocket money selling guava to fruit-preserving companies for three dollars per forty-pound box. Fruit flies also favor this fruit as nurseries for their eggs, so watch for the pinprick marks that betray the presence of maggots. If you intend to seek out this fruit, look for a tree with smooth, tan outer bark that continually peels, revealing light shades beneath it.

Hiking inland you will occasionally glimpse the stream and, in the summer and fall, smell the wafting fragrance of the ginger blossoms. A gentle grade leads to a stand of bamboo and a picnic shelter ¾ mile inland.

Within ½ mile look on the left side of the trail for a misleading stake marked "1 mi." You have not traveled a mile from the beach; however, this stake does mark the first mango tree (see page 28) on the trail. Dominating the left side of the trail, its 2-foot-thick trunk branches up to leaves that are narrow and about 10 inches in length.

About ¼ mile farther inland a magnificent stand of bamboo, or 'ohe (see page 24), towers over the trail; another huge mango tree is on your right, across the trail from the picnic shelter. Taro once grew between two rock walls on this level terrace. The old coffee mill was located just inland of the shelter. Look for its stone stack hidden in the growth to the left of the trail as you proceed inland.

If you wish to trek the last 1¼ mile to the falls, continue inland past a "trail start" marker. In 1982, Hurricane Iwa devastated this portion of the trail; winds of over 80 miles per hour swirled down from the south into the valley head, toppling many of the trees. Look for evidence of this destruction as you make your way up to the falls.

The trail crosses more terraces as it leads through the guava thickets. Taro was grown in level paddies flooded by a sophisticated system of irrigation ditches, or *'auwai,* that diverted stream water to these terraces. Hawai'i's first Western visitors made note in their journals of the natives' expertise in irrigation. Although Hawaiians grew taro in deep mud to allow the development of sizable corms (roots), taro still grows wild along the stream beds.

Taro was the most important plant in Hawaiian culture, so, according to ritual, men cultivated the taro crop while women tended to the sweet potatoes. Taro originally came to Hawai'i with the first Polynesian settlers on their double-hulled canoes. Mythology recounts that the deities Papa and Wakea (Mother Earth and Father Sky, respectively) buried their first-born outside their hut and the child grew into the first taro plant.

The heart-shaped leaves of the taro plant, called *lū'au,* grow 12 to 18 inches long and resemble spinach when cooked. Unlike spinach, however, *lū'au* cannot be eaten raw. Like its relative, dumb cane *(Dieffenbachia),* the entire taro plant contains calcium oxalate crystals that irritate the mouth and feel like tiny needles if eaten. Cooking makes the calcium-rich root and leaves edible—a boon for the Hawaiians who had no dairy products. In the 1800s taro was exported along with coffee from Hanakāpī'ai.

Coffee still abounds in this part of the valley, so look for it shortly after you start the falls trail. Its leaves, 5 inches long and glossy green, have a distinct ruffle along the edge. Depending on the time of year, the plant sports either white blossoms or red berries along its branches. The fragrant blossoms are a reminder that coffee is closely related to the gardenia.

The process that takes the red berries to your coffee cup entails stripping the flesh from the seed then drying the seeds for about a week before roasting them. Five pounds of berries yield a pound of coffee ready to be ground and brewed. Wild beans do, however, tend to be bitter.

Hanakāpī'ai Falls

It is necessary to ford Hanakāpī'ai Stream three times before reaching the falls. Mountain apple trees (see page 25) and yam vines (page 26) cover the valley below the first stream crossing, ¼ mile from the "trail start" marker near the coffee mill site. Beyond this point a small cousin of the *hala*, *'ie'ie* (see page 24), twines itself around the trees.

The trail crosses the stream a second time, just over 1 mile from the start, at a large, deep pool. For swimming, this pool offers a safe alternative to the plunge pool at the falls, where water is captured from a waterfall 120 feet high. The pool at the falls is inviting yet dangerous, owing to rocks falling from the cliffs overhead. This problem is illustrated by the sharp shards of rock that surround the pool. People have been injured in the past, so be alert and do not linger in the fallout zone beneath the cliff any longer than necessary.

You might notice small rocks wrapped in *ti* leaves along the trail and near the pool. An old-timer taught me to leave one of these symbolic offerings to Kamapua'a, the pig demigod, who could turn himself from a pig to a man at will. Many Hawaiian myths describe his unsuccessful attempts to woo Pele. Pele spurned him, touching off numerous contests of power and wit between the two. Legends depict Kamapua'a as a prankster; the *ti*-leaf offerings keep him from throwing stones down on hikers in the narrow valleys. I think of this tradition of making an offering as added insurance, but please spare our *ti* plants.

After the third stream crossing, turn around and look 10 feet above the stream. A sill of dense lava, 3½ feet thick, angles 20 degrees upwards toward the falls. Basically, sills are the horizontal equivalent of the dikes that help to form freshwater springs.

I always find a swim at the waterfall worthwhile, although the water might appear dirty and your limbs will take on a jaundiced yellow tinge when you submerge them. As rainwater trickles through the leaf litter in the forest above, it steeps just like tea. The tannin that gives both tea and this pool its rich color is an excellent softener for your hair and skin, so plunge in! Amazingly, the same tannin that soothes your skin also accelerates the rate of erosion of the cliffs above you. Also known as tannic acid it chemically decays rock; the rock is then washed away by the water.

ON TO HANAKOA

#9   Between the 2½ and 3 mile markers you pass two exposed layers of dense lava rock, each of which is about 15 feet thick. Half a mile farther along the trail, maidenhair fern (a) grows on a black cliff, irrigated by a constant trickle of water. One May I spotted a rare endemic hibiscus *(H. saintjohnianus)* blooming along this portion of the trail. This type of hibiscus grows nowhere else on earth except along this coast. You might see the tangerine-colored blossoms of this hibiscus if you watch for it carefully.

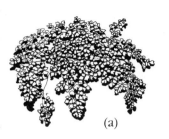

#10

Just before the 3¼ mile marker, where the trail passes between the cliff and a large boulder, your sweating brow tells you that you have climbed to the highest point along the Kalalau Trail—a great place to rest. If you are not acrophobic but fool-hardy, like myself, walk around the side of the boulder to look down to the glistening sea 800 feet below.

(a)

Wave action formed this sheer rock face by gradually carving out a cave at sea level and enlarging it until the cave collapsed. Each successive winter's surf deepens the remaining bowl. Three smaller caves are visible from the ocean—an impressive sight with the vault of bare rock above it.

If the view of the peaceful cove below gives you vertigo, prop yourself up on the west side of the boulder and relish the view of the cliffs rising from sea level up to Pōhākea 3,400 feet above. This view into Hoʻolulu Valley is my secret favorite; the clouds swirling around the cliffs above remind me of a Chinese painting. The scene lacks only a little old man poling his skiff through the stream.

For the next 2¼ miles the trail leads you through Hono O Nā Pali, a State Natural Area Reserve. The state's eighteen reserves protect patches of Hawaiʻi's native ecosystem that remain intact. Together, Hoʻolulu and Waiahuakua valleys represent one of the last strongholds of Hawaiʻi's lowland native forest. The Natural Area Reserves system includes a spectrum of forests, grasslands, bogs, lakes, sand dunes, and marine environments. Unlike the State Parks system, which focuses on recreation, only hiking, hunting, and photography are allowed in the reserves. Rules prohibit any activity that is destructive to the environment, including tent camping and fires.

Hoʻolulu Valley

Like the name Honolulu, Hoʻolulu means "protected bay or waters." Here the name very likely refers to the cove directly beneath the trail's high point. A lack of archaeological remains indicates that Hawaiians did not live in Hoʻolulu Valley, although canoes traveling up the coast rested in the lee of the cove below.

From this vantage point note where the trail exits the far side (west) of the valley, 200 feet below your current elevation. Listen for an unusual squeaking chatter above you coming from Hawaiʻi's most

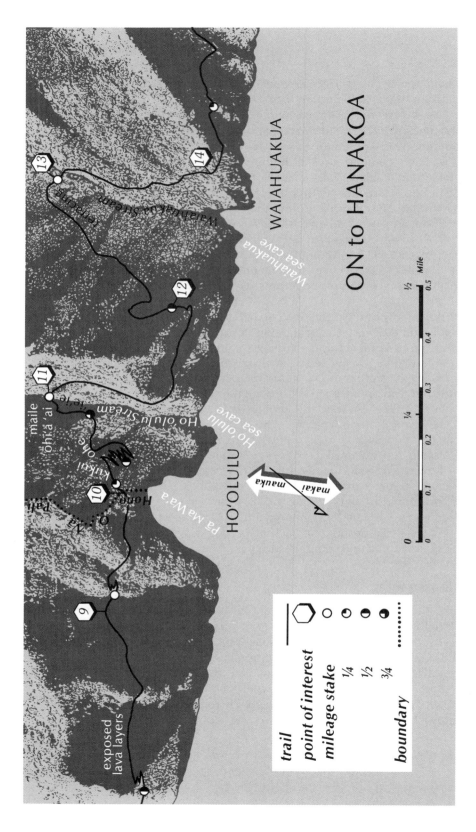

ON to HANAKOA

WAIAHUAKUA

Waiahuakua sea cave

Waiahuakua Stream

terrace

13

14

12

11

maile

ʻōhiʻa ʻai

lehua

Hoʻolulu Stream

ʻōhiʻa

Kukui

10

Hono ʻO

Hono

Pā Mawaʻa

ʻAʻa Pali

9

exposed
lava layers

Hoʻolulu sea cave

HOʻOLULU

mauka

makai

trail

point of interest

mileage stake

¼

½

¾

boundary

0   0.1   0.2   0.3   0.4   0.5

¼   ½   Mile

graceful seabird, the white-tailed tropic bird; with its foot-long white tail feathers streaming out behind its 2-foot wingspan, the name describes the bird well. During their breeding season the *koaʻe,* as the natives call them, nest in the lava cliffs above the trail. I delight in watching them soar on the updrafts, flitting in and out of crevasses in the rock where they eventually lay a single egg. Hawaiians ate *koaʻe* and used their tail plumage to decorate royal standards, called *kahili.*

Other seabirds frequent the coastline during the spring and summer breeding season. Although seabirds can live at sea indefinitely—eating fish and squid, the need to lay eggs and raise their chicks brings them back to land.

Another impressive seabird that you are likely to see along the coast is the frigate bird, or *ʻiwa.* These prehistoric-looking black birds glide on wings spanning 7 feet. They are, however, freaks of nature; although the *ʻiwa* lives its life at sea its wings lack the oil coating required by water birds, so it must not get drenched. To compensate for this handicap they have developed a behavior that has earned them the name of *manu ʻiwa,* literally meaning  "thief bird." *ʻIwas* wait in the wings while other seabirds fish, then swoop down and scare their victim into dropping or even regurgitating their prey, which then becomes the *manu ʻiwa*'s meal. Hawaiians, in turn, preyed upon the *ʻiwa* for food, and decorated their idols and *kahili* with its glossy black feathers.

I highly recommend a visit to Kauaʻi's Kilauea Lighthouse, a National Wildlife Refuge dedicated to protecting seabird nesting sites. In addition to the frigates and white-tailed tropic birds commonly seen at the lighthouse, a colony of red-tailed tropic birds nests there.

Hoʻolulu Valley was formed in a fashion typical of valleys along the Nā Pali Coast. Since the last volcanic eruptions, rainfall runoff whittling down the lava as well as surf cutting away the seaward edge of the valley have carved a hanging valley, where the floor is well above sea level. In Hoʻolulu Valley the floor sits about 200 feet above the sea. Only one valley along the trail, Hanakāpīʻai, slopes gradually to sea level. The presence of hanging valleys accounts for the lack of nice beaches along this section of Kauaʻi's coastline.

Not far around the corner, at the 3¼ mile marker, stop and notice how the goats have nibbled the *ti* plants along the trail, leaving only the tattered stalks.

The trail passes through a grove of *kukui* trees, their maple-shaped leaves littering the ground beneath them. From a distance the distinctively colored, light gray-green leaves stand out against the deeper green foliage of the forest. Hawai'i chose *kukui* as its state tree because the Hawaiians valued every part of it: wood, nuts, and sap. They used the wood for building hut frames and as fuel for their *imu*. In spite of the wood's softness, the Hawaiians fashioned the *kukui* trunk into a canoe, gluing the gunwales on with the tree's sap.

The nickname of the *kukui,* candlenut tree, refers to the nut's oily kernel, which was a source of light for the Hawaiians. Roasted and strung together, each nut (a) burns for about six minutes. Although the raw nut acts as a strong purgative, the Hawaiians ate small quantities roasted with rock salt as a condiment. Eaten raw, the nuts can elicit a strong allergic response, so do not experiment with them. Dyes for *tapa* cloth also came from charred *kukui* nut kernels and locals still wear leis made from the glossy black nutshells. For lei-making, ingenious natives drilled holes in the nuts, then buried the nuts until insects ate away the kernel. Now high-speed drills do this job.

(a)

After the 3¼ mile marker, the trail zigzags down into the valley, then heads inland to cross the stream at an elevation of 400 feet. You can familiarize yourself with a few more forest plants in this area. Shortly after crossing the stream you will see the long, smooth green stalks of the bamboo (b). The Hawaiians call this relative of sugar cane *'ohe,* and fashioned musical instruments from segments of the stalk. Two bamboo percussion instruments kept time for hula dancing: the *pu'ili,* or split bamboo, and *ka'eke'eke,* or stomping tubes. The Hawaiians also made a bamboo flute that is played by exhaling through the nose rather than the mouth.

(b)

In the back of Ho'olulu Valley you might notice a vine resembling *hala* twined around trees. Like *hala,* this vine—called *'ie'ie* (c)—belongs to the screwpine family. *'Ie'ie* is one of the few plants in the world that has its flowers pollinated by a mammal instead of birds or bees. Rats carry pollen from male to female trees

(c)

while feasting on the bright orange fruit. Hawaiians fashioned the fibrous stalk of the *'ie'ie* plant into baskets, nets, and the framework for the feathered helmets worn by warriors. They also used the plant to decorate hula altars.

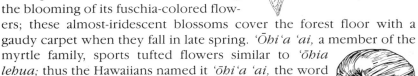

At the back of Hoʻolulu Valley you will pass the 4 mile marker along the trail. Nearby grows a tall tree, the *'ōhi'a 'ai,* that bears the edible mountain apple. Its fruit ripen in the late summer following the blooming of its fuschia-colored flow-   #11
ers; these almost-iridescent blossoms cover the forest floor with a gaudy carpet when they fall in late spring. *'Ōhi'a 'ai,* a member of the myrtle family, sports tufted flowers similar to *'ōhia lehua;* thus the Hawaiians named it *'ōhi'a 'ai,* the word *'ai* describes it as a food plant. The deep red fruit are juicy although not too flavorful. Natives steeped *'ōhi'a 'ai* bark to make a tea to cure sore throats.

A fragrant vine, *maile,* grows along this segment of the trail. Its dark green leaves grow 1 to 2 inches long and the fruit resemble small black olives. The *maile* that grows on Kauaʻi is the least pungent of that growing elsewhere in the islands. The goddess of hula, Laka, took the form of *maile,* so hula dancers adorned both themselves and the *halau hula* with leis made of *maile.* Hawaiian chiefs symbolized a truce by intertwining two *maile* strands.

Leaving Hoʻolulu Valley you can see Kēʻē Beach behind you as well as the sheer drop below the trail's high point. The next valley, Waiahuakua, is less than ½ mile from the back of Hoʻolulu Valley.

Waiahuakua Valley

Just shy of the 4½ mile marker you have your first view of Waiahuakua   #12
Valley. This valley shares its name with the 3,800-foot-high peak inland and west of the valley.

The most spectacular sea cave along the coast lies in the cove below you. Over the eons Waiahuakua Stream cut down through the roof of a sea cave where it now splashes into the sea below. Sunlit water stream-ing down into the dark cave makes a memorable sight for boaters in the summer. The trail follows the 600-foot contour into the valley, switching back once before it continues to the back of the valley.

A complex system of agricultural terraces, some visible from the trail, covers the valley bottom. However, no house sites have been located during recent archaeological surveys.

#13   At the 5-mile point you cross the main branch of the stream. The same vegetation you passed in Ho'olulu Valley grows in Waiahuakua Valley: mountain apple trees *('ōhi'a 'ai)* abound near the stream, and yam vines spiral their way up the tree trunks in the spring and summer months. The Hawaiians did not cultivate this inedible wild yam, called *pi'oi* on Kaua'i. The walnut-sized tubers on this vine are poisonous if not properly cooked, so natives used them only as famine food.

The Hawaiians did eat two other varieties of yams and traded the more popular variety, called *uhi,* to sea captains, who found them suitable for their ships' stores. *Uhi* grows in the wet regions of Kaua'i, such as the Nā Pali Coast. The vines of this seasonal food crop die back in winter, after the fall harvest.

#14   As the trail leads out along the western slope of Waiahuakua Valley it drops below 400 feet above sea level—the lowest point on the trail since Hanakāpī'ai. You can look across the valley to where you entered on the eastern ridge and see the trail 200 feet above you.

The last stretch of trail before Hanakoa Valley follows a series of dips in and out above the sea. Here *hala* trees provide shade in the summer. During the winter months, with the sun far south, this area lies in shadow most of the day. After the 5½ mile marker there are two switchbacks and a short grade before the trail abruptly crests at a ridge. Here, at Hanakoa Valley, you leave Hono O Nā Pali and reenter Nā Pali Coast State Park. The view from the ridge is worth stopping to enjoy, since it will be your last view of the coast until you exit Hanakoa Valley on the west side.

HANAKOA VALLEY

Hanakoa Valley, like its smaller neighbor, Waiahuakua, is a hanging valley with no beach. To save precious elevation, the trail follows the 500-foot contour through the valley rather than descending to sea level.

#15   As you walk inland along the path a clearing on the right (west) side of the trail offers an excellent view of the valley. This bluff was a helipad until 1981, when commercial helicopter landings were banned in the park. However, occasionally helicopters land here to drop off park personnel who do routine maintenance.

Two large waterfalls grace the cliffs before you: the one on the right (west) is a part of Hanakoa Stream, and the one to the left is Hanakoa

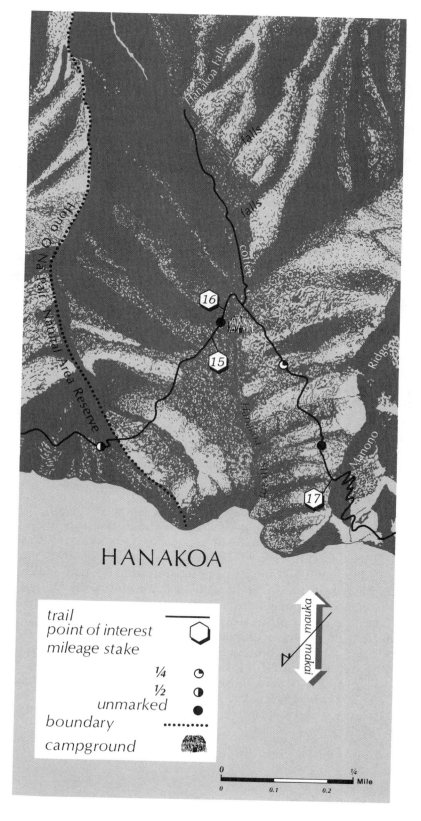

Hanakoa falls

falls

falls

coffee

Hono O Na Pali Natural Area Reserve

16

15

Halihali stream

Manono Ridge

17

HANAKOA

trail
point of interest
mileage stake
¼
½
unmarked
boundary
campground

mauka

makai

N

0   ¼
Mile
0   0.1   0.2

Falls—less than a mile's walk behind the camp area. The remote location of Hanakoa Falls means that you can often enjoy its splendor in solitude. Most weary hikers forego the extra 40-minute walk to Hanakoa Falls, which is similar to the waterfall at Hanakāpī'ai.

The translation of the name Hanakoa typifies the ambiguity in many Hawaiian place names. In Hawaiian, *hana* can mean either "work" or "bay," while *koa* refers to the *koa* tree or to warriors. Samuel H. Elbert and Mary K. Pukui, authorities on the Hawaiian language, translate Hanakoa to mean "bay of the koa tree" or "bay of the warriors," although I have never heard a satisfactory explanation for either meaning.

Archaeological evidence indicates extensive habitation and cultivation in the Hanakoa Valley by Hawaiian natives. An 1835 census tallied fifty Hawaiians living in Hanakoa. When the Hawaiians abandoned taro cultivation, they modified the terraced walls around the taro paddies for growing coffee bean trees (see page 19). Most of the campsites still nestle among wild coffee plants, and as you get closer to the stream you will walk up over small terrace walls.

As you walk inland past the 6 mile marker, level terraces on your right offer suitable campsites. Some of these sites sit in the presence of grand, old mango trees: if you took the hike to Hanakāpī'ai Falls you might already be familiar with this tree, which is native to India. The presence of these aged mango trees usually indicates former sites of Hawaiian habitation, as the natives quickly added this tasty introduced fruit to their diet.

#16   Prior to crossing Hanakoa Stream you pass an old shack on the left-hand side of the trail where you might be welcomed by a feline greeting committee. These stray cats live off of handouts and out of unattended backpacks, so beware. Hunters and hikers have used this shack over the years, yet it is slowly being dismantled by time and offers little protection from the rain—much less from the hungry hordes of mosquitoes that haunt Hanakoa. Hanakoa has no *lua,* so get out your trowel. Be sure to dig your own *lua* at least 6 inches deep and 50 feet or more from the stream to avoid contaminating this source of drinking water.

You will find a delightful swimming hole down a short trail directly west (right) of the shack. It makes a refreshing end to the 6-mile hike. For more private bathing facilities you can boulder-hop upstream of the crossing, where you will find an effervescent pool.

There are more campsites on the far side of the stream. Camping on the narrow spit of land that divides the two forks of the stream can be dangerous. During rainy periods this area floods and it is easy to be stranded here. As you climb up from the stream bed you will find several campsites among the coffee bean trees on your left.

You will quickly notice that in addition to its wealth of coffee the valley also boasts an impressive resident mosquito population. Before you set up your tent or strip down for a swim a little repellent might be in order if mosquitoes find you as delectable as they do me.

If you wonder how the Hawaiians tolerated the constant irritation of these mosquitoes, the answer is that before the arrival of foreigners they did not have to. Mosquitoes were one of the "gifts" that the whaling ships delivered to the islands. While replenishing their water supplies on the island of Maui, the crew of the visiting ship dumped the larvae-laden dregs from their water casks into a stream. Experts are able to tell which ports in South America were visited by these ships based on the type of mosquitoes introduced to Hawaii. These insects quickly spread to all of the islands, forcing natives to move from the luxuriant jungle valleys to the breezier coastlines. Luckily we were not "blessed" with the anopheles mosquito, which carries malaria.

Interestingly, mosquitoes live primarily off plant juices, and only the females bite in order to obtain the protein necessary for reproduction. If they cannot get blood they are forced to sacrifice the protein in their wings.

Hanakoa Falls

After crossing the stream, the trail to Hanakoa Falls branches off *mauka* from the Kalalau Trail. Look for the fork at the first campsite, which sits atop a walled terrace. The trail dips down to cross the western fork of the stream, branches left, then works its way back to the eastern fork of the stream. The trail follows a steep slope with poor footing, so proceed cautiously. Less than ½ mile inland you will come to the falls.

For a mile past Hanakoa Stream the Kalalau Trail follows a gentle grade up out of Hanakoa Valley. At the 7-mile point the trail crosses over Manono Ridge, offering a sweeping view along the coast. #17

At Manono Ridge the coastline curves imperceptibly to the south—yet is enough of a shift in direction to change the whole complexion of the rest of the trail. This bend in the island's shoreline shields the rest of the coast from the tradewind clouds, resulting in lighter rainfall. On many occasions I have waited at Kalalau Beach for a rain squall that seemed to be blowing down from Hanakoa. Instead the clouds moved out to sea from Manono Ridge, taking the rain with them. It is not unusual to see clouds streaming out to sea from the ridge where you now stand.

In the 1890s farmers loaded coffee into boats anchored in the cove to the east of where you stand on the ridge. During calm weather they reportedly dropped sacks of coffee beans from the rock ledge onto shore boats, then transported the sacks out to a larger vessel lying off-shore.

Before you leave Manono Ridge look for an orange, string-like plant growing in the area. *Kauna'oa,* a sinister native vine, derives nutrients from other plants by attaching a series of suckers to its victim. Its leaves, no longer needed to produce food, have evolved into tiny scales. This parasite has been known to go so far as to cannibalize itself. A lei of this dodder, as *kauna'oa* is also known, represents the island of Lāna'i.

Another botanical oddity flourishing in this area is the air plant, so called because it seemingly lives on air. You can sprout new plants by simply hanging an air plant leaf from a curtain rod. The plant is about 2 feet tall and has scalloped leaves that sprout from one main stem and pinkish blossoms that hang like clusters of tiny Chinese lanterns. The poisonous leaves protect the air plant from hungry goats, thus insuring its survival along the coast. Natives in other tropical regions where this plant also thrives make these leaves into cool compresses for fevers.

Zigzagging down the western slope of Manono Ridge you walk though a thick stand of sisal, the same plant that you encountered hiking out of Hanakāpī'ai Valley. The trail descends to an elevation of only 200 feet above sea level—its lowest point between Hanakāpī'ai and Kalalau.

Be forewarned that from here on goat and pig hunters use rifles. Regulations limit pig hunting to weekends only, and goat hunting is restricted to eight weekends in late summer (see page 74).

HANAKOA TO KALALAU

Notice the numerous changes in the character of the coastline beyond Manono Ridge. The lighter rainfall combined with the drying effect of the wind, winter sea spray, and the large number of goats conspire to change the landscape. Now you will be hiking in and out of small gullies rather than the large valleys cut by plentiful rainfall that dominated the first portion of the trail.

Vegetation here is sparse, and only hardy, low-lying scrub does well on the exposed ridges. Even in the protected gullies plants grow less luxuriantly than they did east of Hanakoa. These harsh growing conditions give erosion the upper hand. Plants cannot grow quickly enough to cover areas where goats or landslides have stripped the vegetation from the earth and left bare, red scars on the land. However, this barren landscape does reveal clues about the geological formation of the Nā Pali Coast and makes it easy to spot goats as well as archaeological sites along the trail.

After you pass the low point the trail climbs and turns inland to cross two small gullies, the second of which has a running brook. Entering on the east side, stop to look up at the far ridge; the creek that cut this ravine has exposed two dikes. These dikes run parallel to each other, angling inland slightly as they rise upward. You might remember that such dikes account for the springs that you pass en route to Hanakāpī-'ai. These intrusions of dense rock form the walls of Hawai'i's natural water tanks, which release their water in the form of springs.

As you watch your footfall on the trail, notice the changes in the earth. Where earlier you walked around mud puddles and over rich, brown soil, you now hike over crumbly red dirt. As rich as it looks, this rotten red rock lacks humus, the decayed plant material needed for plants to thrive. Wetter sections of the coast, like Hanakāpī'ai, have more vegetation and therefore more humus in the soil, which accounts for the richer brown color.

Iron gives the soil a red hue as it rusts, or oxidizes. Unfortunately, the iron in this rich-looking soil is not in a form that plants can use. The first pineapple growers in Hawai'i made this discovery and were astounded to find that their plants were starved for iron when they could *see* the iron oxide in the soil. Now they add soluble iron to the soil for healthy plant growth.

As you approach the next gully look for a 30-foot-thick layer of dark gray rubble overlain by red earth. If you travel down the coast by boat you will pass an arch that formed where the ocean wore through one such layer. Onionskin boulders litter the slope above this gully. The process of weathering gradually peels away layers of lava rock from around these boulders, much like peeling an onion. For millions of years lava has been

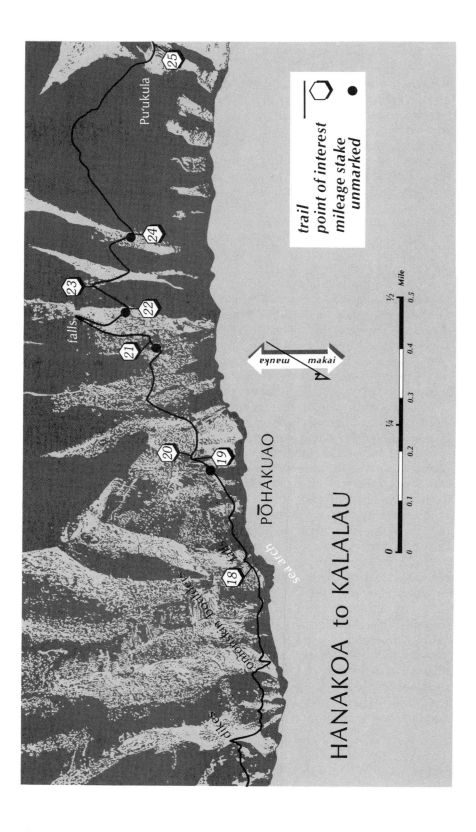

HANAKOA to KALALAU

Purukula

PŌHAKUAO

falls

search

boulder

toumbskin border

dikes

trail
point of interest
mileage stake
unmarked

mauka   makai

0   0.1   1/4   0.3   0.4   1/2   Mile
     0.2   0.5

decaying, while rainstorms wash away the resulting loose soil, leaving these boulders behind.

As you hike keep in mind that you are walking over lava laid down millions of years ago; what appears to be solid rock underfoot often crumbles treacherously. A member of a well-known local family, while leading an expedition into Nā Pali, reportedly said that hikers wearing tennis shoes might as well throw themselves over the cliffs at the beginning of the trip, since they would eventually lose their footing wearing such flimsy footwear on this crumbly soil.

Pōhakuao

You now walk through an ancient Hawaiian land division named Pōhakuao. Of five such land divisions—or *ahupua'a*—along this coast, Pōhakuao, located between Hanakoa and Kalalau valleys, is the smallest. Each *ahupua'a* had a *konohiki,* or steward, who looked after the interests of the island's chief. In terms of land management these chiefs were similar to the feudal lords of Europe in the Middle Ages.

Late each fall natives piled a myriad of goods from each district at the boundary of the *ahupua'a* to be collected by the chief's tax collectors; for the ancient Hawaiians this event was equivalent to our April 15. It is likely that tribute from Pōhakuao included fishnets and feathered cloaks made from the hemplike *olonā* plant that grew in the area. *Olonā* was later grown commercially in Pōhakuao, as its fiber has greater strength than that of hemp.

Hawaiians once cultivated taro on the level area halfway between Manono Ridge and Kalalau Valley. From the western edge of this bluff   #18 Kalalau Beach looks deceptively close, but 3 miles of winding trail lie between you and your destination.

After climbing up out of the next gully look down at the ocean directly beneath you to see the sea arch mentioned earlier. The trail leads along a steep, grassy slope where you can easily imagine cattle grazing as they did in the middle of this century. The goat population still keeps this area nicely mowed.

At the next stream crossing you will find *'ape* growing. Its immense, heart-shaped leaves resemble mutant taro leaves that somehow quadrupled in size as the result of some science experiment that went awry. At mid-day shiny black lizards bask on the rocks in this ravine. These lizards, called skinks, seldom exceed 4 inches in length and are one of the two most common types of lizards

#19

found in Hawai'i, geckos being the other. The skinks work the day shift in Hawai'i, while geckos proclaim their nighttime presence with loud "chirps." Geckos can change the shade of their skin from off-white to  charcoal brown, while a skink's snake-like scales remain metallic
#20   black.

Where the trail switches back up from this ravine, a rock wall 2½ feet high follows the path for about 12 feet. You can easily examine the technique used in building these terracing walls. The Hawaiians were remarkable stonemasons—instead of using mortar in their walls they relied on the careful placement of each rock to give the wall its strength.

From this bluff the trail curves inland across one of the seven gulches that make up Pōhakuao. These narrow, flood-prone valleys, not suitable for growing taro, forced the Hawaiians to reverse their normal settlement pattern along the coast. Archaeological evidence indicates that although the Hawaiians lived near the gullies, they built *'auwai* around to the level bluffs to irrigate their crops.

You now begin to gain the 500 feet of elevation necessary to take you up over Red Hill and into Kalalau Valley. Sisal and lantana line this section of trail. You can recognize the ambitious weed, lantana, by the clusters of miniature yellow and orange flowers that decorate much of the trail. Lantana leaves resemble those of its relative, mint, and like many members of this family its leaves give off a pungent aroma when crushed.

Elsewhere in the world lantana grows as an ornamental shrub, and it was brought to Kaua'i at the turn of the century for that purpose. Birds soon took a liking to the juicy lantana fruit and so spread its seeds far and wide. In our tropical climate lantana grows to the size of a small tree. Having hiked many miles through its clawlike thorns I could not resist making a sarcastic remark when I spied lantana growing in the Boston Gardens.

Proceeding up through the colony of sisal plants, look for the new plants that have fallen from their lofty nurseries. After dropping these sprouts the stalk dries out; split in half, these were popular for fencing material when I was a girl. Now these stalks topple over and decay, as if some giant has just left his game of pick-up sticks.

#21   The trail continues to wend its way upward and inland, crossing another stream before a long ascent up the eastern slope of the next ridge. A remnant of a terracing wall 7 feet high still stands *mauka* of the stream crossing. Did the rest of the wall wash away during flooding over the years, leaving only this triangular patch of stonework?

The trail climbs up the side of this vale in the shade of the *kukui* trees that have paved the path with their black nutshells. Keep an eye out for the bend where the trail zigs back to the right; rocks are placed across the path to prevent hikers from mistakenly going straight instead of turning right. A small waterfall trickles down a 10-foot-high rock face at this juncture, making it a refreshing place to refill your water bottle. As a precaution I recommend purifying this water before drinking it.

Stop on the next ridgeline to enjoy the view and fresh breeze. Look- #22
ing *makai* along the ridge to your left (west) you will see two large *pukas*, or holes, in the rock. The vivid blue sea showing through the black and red lava cliff makes a stunning picture on a summer day.

Dipping back *mauka* you pass again into the shade and find yet an- #23
other vestige of the ranching era along Nā Pali. Strands of wire from an old fence lie embedded in the trunk of a *kukui* tree that cowboys from Makaweli Ranch "lassoed"; the Robinsons of Ni'ihau fame ran cattle here until the 1970s. Happily for your weary body, the next river you cross after this creek will be Kalalau Stream, little more than a mile away.

From the next ridgeline you can look back all the way to Manono #24
Ridge at Hanakoa, where another *puka* pierces the ridge. Perhaps forgotten legends told how some ancient giant threw his spear through the ridge, or how a supernatural bird pecked a peephole in the cliff side. Ahead of you the trail curves around in a long sweep to a small saddle where it disappears behind Ka'a'alahina Ridge.

The knoll that forms the right-hand side of the saddle named Pu'ukula, is now called "Red Hill." If you keep quiet you are almost guaranteed to see goats on this part of the trail. Within 20 minutes you will be standing in the Pu'ukula saddle, reveling in the view of Kalalau and the luxury of the final descent to sea level.

KALALAU VALLEY

From Pu'ukula, Kalalau Valley spreads out at your feet. You can see the #25
beach as well as layers of fluted ridges strung down the coastline to Nu'alolo Kai where a reef juts out 100 yards. The map of Kalalau in the next section of this guide will enable you to pinpoint the two lookouts at the back of Kalalau Valley.

Hike down Ka'a'alahina Ridge slowly. The lure of a cool swim in Kalalau Stream is overwhelming on a hot summer day, but hiking down

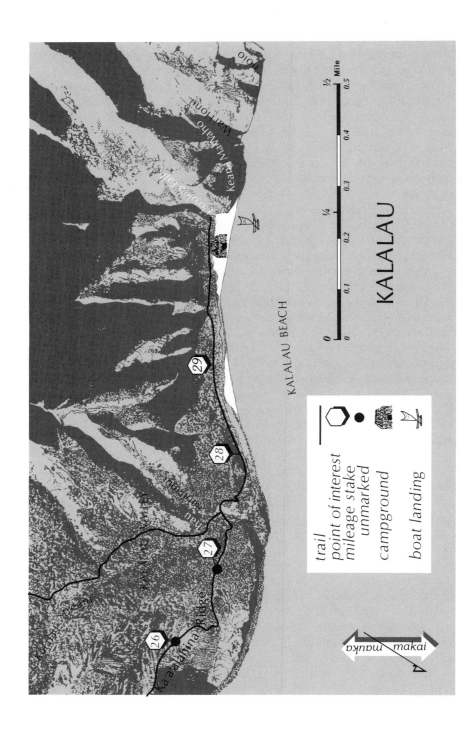

KALALAU

KALALAU BEACH

trail	
point of interest	
mileage stake unmarked	
campground	
boat landing	

mauka makai

Mile
0   0.1   0.2   0.3   0.4   0.5
¼   ½

26 27 28 29

Ka'a'alahina Ridge

store for a pot-luck feast we'll prepare in our cabins tonight. Ready? It's time to drive the spectacular mountain road up to Kokee State Park alongside Waimea Canyon, "The Little Grand Canyon of the Pacific."

Night in cabins @ Kokee State Park   (B)

DAY 8   SAT   JULY 30

If you opt for breakfast at Kokee Lodge, try the macadamia nut/banana pancakes! This is a free day for relaxing, browsing the Kokee Natural History Museum, exploring the hiking trails, and enjoying Kauai's invigorating climate at 4000'. Let's meet at the Lodge this evening for a farewell dinner.

2nd night in cabins @ Kokee

DAY 9   SUN   JULY 31

We'll leave Kokee early and do a little exploring en route to Lihue and our noon flight back to Honolulu. There's lots to do on Oahu--visit the Bishop Museum or Pearl Harbor, sample great international cuisine, explore Diamond Head, hang out on Waikiki Beach, or snorkel at Hanuama Bay. . . If one must return to the mainland, an evening departure is ideal--if it allows us to make the most of our last day in Hawaii and to sleep through the night en route. . .

DAY 10   MON   AUGUST 1

. . . to home. We'll arrive about noon, with daytime to spare.

ALOHA!

REMARKABLE JOURNEYS

KAYAK KAUAI:
The Na Pali Coast!
July 23 - August 1, 1994

Experience six days of spectacular kayaking and snorkeling off Kauai's incredible Na Pali coast... camp and hike the beautiful, remote tropical valleys of Kalalau, Nu'alolo and Miloli'i...explore Kokee State Park's mountain trails from cabins at 4000'...sample great local seafood, Lappert's spectacular ice cream, and Banana Joe's lucious fresh fruit smoothies!

We'll be paddling stable, comfortable sit-on-top sea kayaks with rudders, both tandem and solo boats. North shore waters are normally calm in mid-summer, making this a great trip for beginners in good shape as well as for more experienced paddlers. join us!

DAY 1   SAT   JULY 23
Arrive in Honolulu mid-afternoon. Our inter-island flight to Princeville on Kauai's north shore gives us a great bird's-eye view of this amazing tropical paradise. Enjoy a laid-back afternoon, island-style, then we'll re-group for dinner and discuss tomorrow's paddling plans.
Night camping @ Hanalei

DAY 2   SUN   JULY 24
It's our first day on the water! Our shuttle west along Kauai's lush north coast delivers us to a beach park near the end of the road. Heading out from Haena, we paddle westward *with* the prevailing wind

into a deep-blue ocean fringed with white surf. We'll camp our first two nights at Kalalau beach, our free day devoted to hiking, swimming in shady fresh-water pools, and foraging for wild passion fruit, guava, and papaya. Have you ever imagined Eden? It probably looked like this!

Night camping @ Kalalau

DAY 3   MON   JULY 25

Enjoy a free day exploring Kalalau Valley. . .

2nd night camping @ Kalalau   (B)

DAY 4   TUE - THU   JULY 26 - 28

Beyond the verdant valley of Kalalau lies more incredible coastline, including the arches of Honopu and the azure waters of a volcanic sea cave. Pulling ashore nearby, we'll explore the old fishing village site of Nu'alolo Kai with its rock walls, fresh-water well and ancient heiau. Snorkel here and explore the crystal clear waters alive with dazzling reef fish and green sea turtles. Micco says that if we're lucky, Harvey the white tipped shark might be in town! We'll paddle further west then to the beautiful shell-strewn beach at Miloli'i. There's plenty of time here for beachcombing, swimming, hiking, birdwatching, snorkeling, and frolicking in the waterfalls cascading from the mountains above us.

3rd-5th nights camping @ Miloli'i   (3 B, 1 D)

DAY 7   FRI   JULY 29

It's our last day of kayaking! Our final destination is Polihale State Park where the mountains meet the sand dunes on Kauai's dry west coast. We'll load our gear onto our shuttle, then race off to the nearest Lappert's for some of the best ice cream ever (sorry Blue Bell!). We'll also shop at a well-stocked grocery

P.O. Box 31855 ✧ Houston, Texas 77231-1855
713-721-2517 ✧ Fax 713-728-8334 ✧ Toll Free 800-856-1993

TRIP COST: **$1765 from Houston**   **$1075 from Honolulu**

INCLUDES: inter-island air, ground transport, 6 nights camping, 2 nights lodging, kayaks & paddling gear, local guide, park permits & fees, 5 breakfasts & 1 dinner

Note: This trip is suitable for physically fit individuals with reasonable upper body strength who are comfortable in the water. No previous kayak experience is required.

this crumbly, eroded slope is tricky. Take the time to appreciate the wild hues that result from the weathering of the earth here: few places boast blue dirt.

Halfway down the hill a rusted stub marks the 9½-mile point. On the grassy slope below and to your right are neatly arranged terrace walls. I have been told this was one of the last areas in Kalalau cultivated with taro, although how they brought water around to this area puzzles me. #26

At the bottom of Kaʻaʻalahina Ridge the trail leads a few hundred yards through a windblown stand of Java plum and guava. Here you pass several boulders, some with smooth, 1-inch-wide grooves worn in them. The Hawaiians used these rocks for sharpening their stone implements.

The trail then dips down to cross Kalalau Stream. I seldom cross this stream without intentionally falling in. Usually there is a log and a rope to help hikers get across with dry feet, but somehow that gurgling water is too cool to resist and I have to shed my pack and indulge in a Kalalau baptism. #27

A plant resembling corn grows beside the stream. This yellow ginger (a), a mainstay of Hawaiʻi's lei-making industry, blooms in late summer and fall. Its pale yellow flowers mingle with the sweet smell of the fresh water. You might recall that Hawaiians used the juicy clusters of another wild ginger, *ʻawapuhi,* for shampoo.

(a)

At a junction on the far side of the stream the trail branches left into the valley, while bearing right to the campground and beach. Domestic plants, such as a white-flowered periwinkle (b) and the tomato, welcome you to this civilized bit of wilderness as you travel down a small hill toward the beach. If the tomatoes tempt you, beware of the fatally poisonous apple of Sodom (c) masquerading as a tomato. Nature provides apple of Sodom with vicious thorns as a warning for the unwary who mistake its luscious-looking orange fruit for tomatoes.

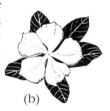

(b)

The trail follows the lower slope of a bluff and offers a stunning view of Kalalau Beach. Hikers arriving in the afternoon find the sea cast in silvery sunlight. A faint trail leads back along the coast behind

(c)

#28

you, below a rock terracing wall. This trail leads to an archaeological site west of Kalalau Stream. Across the stream to the east, the Hawaiians built a *heiau* on a plateau above the sea. When you are not weighted down by a pack and the desire to relax try this worthwhile side trip.

As you walk above the boulder beach the sweet fragrance of be-still might greet you. This tall shrub with yellow blossoms and slender, 5-inch-long leaves grows on the steep slope above you. A member of the periwinkle family and native to tropical America, its poisonous sap, if eaten, can quickly render you lifeless, as its name indicates. Locals also refer to it as yellow oleander.

Congratulations, you have arrived at the trail's end, so treat yourself to a shower or cool drink at Ho'ole'a Falls. The falls, located at the far west end of the beach, is also the social hub of Kalalau. Here campers congregate in the evening to talk while fetching water for dinner and for showers. The Division of State Parks advises hikers to purify drinking water, as goats live above in the small valley through which this stream flows.

The Campsites

Campsites dot the half-mile-long flat above the beach, so keep a lookout for paths leading off to your left into the bush. The summer surf builds the beach out, allowing people to camp in the caves beyond the Ho'ole'a Falls. The westernmost cave collapsed in the spring of 1987 and a rock slide in August of 1980 sealed off the entrance to the next cave east—two good reasons not to camp in those areas. Although convenient, the caves drip water constantly and these "sandboxes" are sometimes used for *lua*.

Social hermits, like myself, prefer the first few sites for the quietude they offer, while those enamored with Ho'ole'a Falls camp at the far west end. The easternmost *lua* is cleaner because fewer people camp nearby, yet you have farther to walk to bathe and fetch water. In addition, take into consideration the level of protection from the sun and wind when choosing a campsite: what appeals to you on a cool, calm morning might be a wretched choice in the broiling afternoon sun and gusty tradewinds. The Division of State Parks limits camping stays at Kalalau to five nights.

You might set up camp under old friends such as the Java plum or *kukui*. Another variety of passion fruit, or *liliko'i,* drapes itself over these trees. The yellow, globular fruit makes a refreshing snack and, unlike the guava with its soft skin, the juicy pulp of *liliko'i* (a) is protected by an inedible, leathery skin. Locals joke that the best time to eat guava is in the dark of night, when its inhabitants cannot be seen. Few people miss the extra protein in the maggot-free passion fruit (b). Despite its name this fruit is not an aphrodisiac; instead zealous Christians named it for the passion of Christ. The passionflower (c) reminded them of a

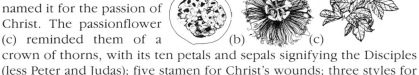

crown of thorns, with its ten petals and sepals signifying the Disciples (less Peter and Judas); five stamen for Christ's wounds; three styles for the three nails; all colored in white and blue for purity and heaven, respectively.

Beautiful *koali 'awa,* a morning glory vine, mingles with the passion fruit. The legend of Pele and Lohi'au continues after the incident at Kē'ē, with Pele leaving Lohi'au in search of a home. In her absence he dies of a broken heart, fearing that she has abandoned him. Pele's sister, Hi'iaka, discovers his soul drifting above Hā'ena, and captures it in a *koali 'awa* blossom. Lohi'au's soul is then returned to his body through a slit in his big toe (a technique

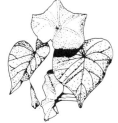

not yet discovered by modern medicine). Poor Lohi'au dies yet again when Pele, realizing that Hi'iaka loves Lohi'au, erupts in anger. Revived by Pele's compassionate brothers, Lohi'au finds life happier the third time around, returning to Kaua'i and a joyous reunion with Hi'iaka.

A walk through the eastern campsites takes you past a cliff where archaeological excavations have been done, as well as past some fine examples of ancient stone walls near the easternmost bathrooms.

In other parts of the world campers hang their food out of the reach of raccoons and bears. In Kalalau the vermin—ants and cockroaches—are much smaller, but what they lack in size they make up for in persistence and number. I found that hanging my food sack from a string impregnated with insect repellent works for a while. If you keep food in your tent be prepared for company. Cats also stalk through the campsites, so take precautions to protect your food.

One of the blessings of this rampant insect population is that it feeds a bevy of birds. Two types of thrush frequent the campsites, literally rustling up dinner: the one wearing olive-drab fatigues and garish white eyeliner is the Chinese thrush (a), while the natty shama thrush (b) sports glossy black coattails and a rosy vest. I unabashedly elect the friendly shama, with its amazing array of songs, as my favorite bird. What a wondrous process transforms cockroaches into such elegant songs! When I am lying in my tent the thrushes thrashing in the leaf litter, searching for cockroaches and other delicacies, sound convincingly like a human intruder.

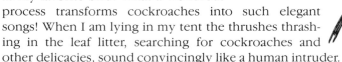

When you have had some time to recuperate from the rigors of the trail, pick up this book again and we can explore Kalalau together.

Kalalau Beach

The same surging winter surf that governs the width of Hanakāpī'ai Beach controls the size of Kalalau Beach. Every winter the swath of sand that stretches from the eastern point past the westernmost cave shrinks to a thin ribbon only 100 yards long, as churning winter waves suck the sand out to sea. Even in the calm summer, a strong current rips westward along the shore, making swimming questionable at best. During the summer you can walk down the beach west of the falls.

In the spring of 1987 a massive landslide destroyed the westernmost cave, which had a small *puka* in the back that lead through to a west-facing beach. The rubble hides your view of Honopū Valley, the next valley around the corner, but on calm days people swim to and from Honopū. This might look tempting, but be advised that a strong current runs westward from the point out to sea and it has carried people away to their final resting place. Evaluate your swimming ability and consider that it is at least five hours out on foot to get help if you get into trouble.

Few shells wash up on Kalalau Beach intact because the surf grinds them up along with coral, making sand. This frustrates many beachcombers bent on taking home a shell from Hawai'i. Local shell collectors dive to find live, whole shells, and those sold in the tourist traps come from the western Pacific. One shell that can be found in abundance is the *'opihi,* which is shaped like a Chinese hat. These edible limpets cling to the boulders at the eastern end of Kalalau Beach and their shells are often littered around campfire rings. Relished as popular *lū'au* fare, *'opihi* sell for about five dollars per pound, although the law forbids taking those smaller than 1¼ inches in diameter. Hawaiians used the larger shells as primitive potato peelers to scrape the skin from taro and sweet potatoes.

The chattering, charcoal-colored birds, *noio,* that live at the west end of Kalalau Beach are common in Nā Pali's numerous sea caves (see page 50).

Strolling back up the beach, take yourself back 200 years to the time when Hawaiians passed the summer hours much the same way as campers do today. They built their *hale* above the falls, where the campsites are now, as well as on the eastern side of Kalalau Valley proper, but in the summer natives slept in the caves, naming the largest one Keana Ma Waho.

Adults spent hours playing a Hawaiian version of checkers in the sand, while west of Keana Ma Waho children splashed in Wai Honu (turtle water), a pool where turtles once laid their eggs. Now the invasion of humanity discourages sea turtles from nesting on Hawai'i's beaches. Children also jumped rope, or *lele koali. Lele* means "to jump" in Hawaiian, and *koali,* you might recall, is the morning glory vine, which they used for their rope.

A shout from a lookout perched on the bluff above would disrupt this placid scene as men grabbed their *ti*-leaf fishing nets and hurried to the shore. Canoes carried out nets to encircle the school of fish that the lookout had spied from above. Soon everyone on shore was pulling *(huki)* in the two ends of the U-shaped, *ti*-leaf *(lau)* dragnet. After the *hukilau,* natives took the catch to the falls to clean them. Lacking refrigeration the Hawaiians salted whatever fish they did not eat right away. Next time you bathe at the falls imagine the joyful ruckus of people cleaning and salting their squirming catch.

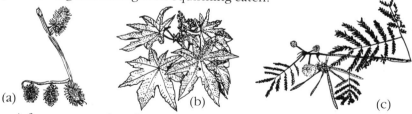

(a)   (b)   (c)

A few noteworthy plants grow around the campsites amid a mix of weeds such as cocklebur (a), castor bean (b), and *koa haole* (c). A grove of *milo* trees shades a cluster of campsites east of the beach as it did the *hale*s of the Hawaiians, who introduced this useful tree. Confined to their grass-thatched *hale* only by rain storms or religious *kapu,* the women preferred sitting out in the shade of *milo* trees to pound mulberry bark into *tapa* cloth. The old men braided a fiber rope from the inner bark of the *milo* tree, whose wood was also made into beautiful bowls.

Papaya, a more recent introduction, grow throughout the campgrounds, although hungry hikers seldom leave any ripe fruit on the trees. This popular fruit tree grows like a palm tree, with its leaves and fruit atop a slender trunk. The tasty fruit contains a digestive enzyme, papain, as well as vitamin C.

The succulent yellow fruit of *noni* may also look temptingly delectable, but a Camembert-like stink betrays its foul taste. Only famine drove the Hawaiians to eat these fruit, yet they brought *noni* here to grow around their *hale*. Why so? Because flesh wounds healed quickly under a poultice of *noni* fruit, and the stem and roots yielded red and yellow dyes. Hawaiian women spent a great deal of time making *tapa*, and so saved time by having their dye sources nearby.

Noni shares an interesting botanical trait with pineapple. Although each *noni* fruit (and, similarly, pineapple) appears to be one fruit it is actually a group of fruit growing together. Tiny white *noni* flowers grow in tight clusters where every flower develops into one fruit. Like a pineapple whose outer skin has been cut away, *noni* have "eyes" representing the individual fruit, each of which produces a seed.

The silvery *pōhinahina,* or beach vitex, a native beachside plant, sends its runners out onto the sand. The silver sheen of its leaves reflects the sunlight. Crush one of these  leaves and smell it. Can you guess what other fragrant-leafed plant it might be related to? *Pōhinahina* belongs to the same family as that ornamental plant of dubious repute, the lantana.

Evening Entertainment

The main event at Kalalau is the sunset. During the winter around five o'clock the sun glances along the ridges behind the beach before shyly sinking into the cliffs above Honopū. When the surf rises and the air thickens with salt, the sun shines down through the serrated ridges and sets off an array of light beams that casts a satin sheen on the surf. Silver manes of spray stream out behind the waves as they arch and break.

In summer the sun sets into the sea, offering a chance to view the green flash, a small, momentary patch of emerald hue that follows the sun into the sea (see page 72).

The staccato silhouettes of seabirds and aerobatic bats perform as the glow of sunset evaporates into night. In spring and summer, seabirds  —mostly wedge-tailed shearwaters—fly east to Kilauea Point to nest in burrows dug with their webbed feet. The wedge shape of their tails makes them easy to pick out. You may hear the braying of another group of shearwaters, the *'a'o,* as they wing their way inland to their mountain nests hidden in *ulube* fern, where the Hawaiians snared them for food.

Occasionally hoary bats flutter above the beach. These bats and the Hawaiian monk seal are the only two land-based mammals native to Hawai'i. All other mammals, unable to fly or swim to Hawai'i depended on man to provide  them with transportation. Once in a while an adventurous monk seal visits Kaua'i's shores, but generally they keep to the tiny, northwestern islands in the Hawaiian chain where, as endangered species, they are protected by law.

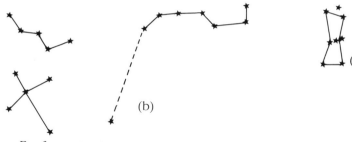

Far from city lights, nightfall brings with it a spectacular planetarium show. Constellations such as Orion (a) and the Big Dipper (b) entertain throughout the night along with the Pleiades (c). Orion guards the winter sky with his starry sword, seemingly driving the Pleiades into the western sea. In Hawaiian mythology the Pleiades star cluster is the heavenly remains of a chief from Kaua'i, Makali'i, who was banished by the pig demigod, Kamapua'a. After defeating Makali'i, Kamapua'a came to Kalalau to visit his parents.

The rising of the star Arcturus ushers in the winter dawn. To find Arcturus, start at the Big Dipper in the northern sky and follow the arc of its handle about two more handle-lengths toward the center of the sky. The Hawaiians called this star *Hōkūle'a,* meaning "clear star." *Hōkūle'a* stands directly over the Hawaiian Islands during summer evenings, and it guided the canoes of the Polynesian settlers from the south to Hawai'i. In the 1970s a sailing canoe named *Hōkūle'a* was successfully navigated between Hawai'i and Tahiti depending solely on Polynesian methods of navigation.

"Going Up Valley"

A popular activity in the morning is to head "up valley" to collect fruit and bathe at Big Pool, a swimming hole 2 miles inland. The trail leads over numerous terraces, through several groves of mango trees, over an open ridge with a superb panorama of the valley, and ends just above Big Pool. Most valley trails are level by nature, but the trail to Big Pool gains 800 feet of elevation. Even if hiking the 11-mile trail from Kē'ē Beach has robbed you of any ambition, the shade and easy grade of this valley trail make it a pleasant half-day trip.

To start the hike to Big Pool retrace your steps to the trail junction near Kalalau Stream, but this time continue *mauka*. You soon pass a tangle of *hau* on your right. This hibiscus tree, the nemesis of many hikers in Hawaii, thrives along stream beds; when bushwacking, its chaotic growth turns a short distance into a grueling struggle. Simply the sight of *hau* is enough to turn me back. *Hau* has round leaves and yellow blossoms that deepen to orange or red with the sunset.

Although a bane to hikers, people throughout Polynesia found many uses for *hau.* Rubbing a stick of hard wood against a piece of soft *hau* produces enough heat to start a fire. Lei makers used the inner fibers of the bark for thread, and the sap and flower have a laxative effect.

The Hawaiians' lives depended on *hau* as a major source of fishing materials. After hollowing out specially selected *koa* trees in the forest, natives dragged these logs to the shore using thick ropes of braided *hau* fiber. From a single *koa* tree weighing upwards of two tons the Hawaiians fashioned one fishing canoe.

The lack of metal in Hawai'i forced canoe builders to shape their canoes with stone adzes lashed onto handles of perfectly curved *hau* branches. Buoyant *hau* wood makes excellent outriggers for stabilizing these narrow canoes and is still used today. Small segments of the *hau* branch also make perfect floats for fishnets—the soft core of the branch is easily removed, making a hole for tying the segments to the net.

To maintain a healthy fish population Hawaiian chiefs periodically placed a *kapu* on reef fishing during spawning seasons; to alert the people in areas where fishing was *kapu, hau* branches were placed along the shoreline.

Missionaries built a school in the area above Kalalau Stream, but the vigorous plant growth has since devoured its remains. A large agricultural *heiau* named Kahuanui also lies buried in the brush west of here. A magnificent example of a *ho'oulu'ai,* as they called their agricultural *heiau,* lies farther down the coast at Nu'alolo Kai (see page 66).

The trail next opens onto an eroded slope, where onionskin boulders sit stripped of the surrounding dirt. On the upper lip of the valley, *mauka,* you can see the two scenic lookouts at the road's end in Kōke'e. Looking back, above Ho'ole'a Falls you can see a *puka* in Kalāhū Ridge (*kalāhū* means "overflowing sun").

More *hau* grows on the far side of the next small stream bed that you cross. Keep an eye out for terracing walls where the trail levels off under a canopy of Java plum. As many as four levels extend both above and below the trail. How different it must have looked before trees and brush took over the abandoned taro patches. Mentally uproot these introduced trees and replant these terraces with taro gently swaying in the sunshine. In 1847 close to 200 people still lived in the *ahupua'a* of Kalalau, their *hale* scattered among the taro patches.

Residents of Kalalau exported whatever taro they did not need, loading ten or more sacks of taro root into a *kukui* wood canoe. Although *kukui* was not the preferred wood for canoe building it was readily available in Kalalau. Four paddlers were needed to make the journey up the coast to trade their crop for other staples. Athletic natives also packed *ōkolehao,* a liquor made from *ti* root, up the cliff to Kōke'e for trade. After the last Hawaiian family moved out of Kalalau in 1919, Makaweli Ranch used the area until the late 1970s to raise cattle. After the late 1970s the state bought the last private lands in Kalalau.

The trail leads past an orange tree, then crosses a small creek. Bear right as you climb up the far side of this stream bed. Be-still and apple of Sodom can be found here.

Within ½ mile you come to an open ridge offering a magnificent view of the entire valley. Looking seaward, note how the horizon lines up with Pu'ukula; this view indicates that you have climbed as high as Pu'ukula—500 feet.

To your right, as you face *mauka,* the rock remains of two children stand high on the ridge. Against their father's orders, Nākeikianā'i'iwi, "the children of the *i'iwi* bird," dallied too long at the shore where they had  gone to fetch water from a special spring. As the sun rose its rays caught them scurrying home and turned them into stone as their father looked on, horrified.

Across Kalalau Valley, on its eastern slope, look for an exposed dike on the fourth major ridge inland. See how the earth on the *makai* side of this dike has washed away, leaving the black wall of dense rock? You can follow the same dike quite a distance up the valley wall. One mile inland, but hidden from view, Waimakemake Falls tumbles down the cliff where Koʻolau the leper hid out in the 1890s.

The outbreak of leprosy in Hawaii forced lepers from Kauaʻi to seek refuge in Kalalau Valley in the 1870s. A law passed five years earlier required that all lepers be shipped to Molokaʻi, but banned family members free of the disease from going along. This meant that husbands would never again see their wives and parents were separated from their children.

In an attempt to stay with their loved ones a band of lepers and their families hid from authorities in Kalalau. Only one family succeeded. In 1892, Koʻolau, a cowboy from Waimea, and his son, Kaleimanu, were diagnosed as having the dreaded disease, although Koʻolau's wife, Piʻilani, was not. In June of 1893 Deputy Sheriff Louis Stolz from Waimea led an attempt to round up and deport eight of the lepers in Kalalau, but by nine o'clock on the evening of June 27, Stolz lay dead, shot by Koʻolau, a man he had once hunted with.

Deputy Sheriff W. E. H. Deverill, the coffee grower from Hanakāpī-ʻai, arrived four days later along with 80 other police and soldiers determined to capture the remaining lepers. For a while Koʻolau hid on a ledge above the spring-fed falls, but slipped away in the night before his pursuers fired nineteen rounds from a howitzer at the ledge. After shooting one other man, Koʻolau finally evaded their attempts to capture him.

For the next two years, Koʻolau and his family hid out in the valley, leading a primitive life until the death of both Koʻolau and his son. After the heart-wrenching death of her husband and child, Piʻilani, faithful to the end, hiked up out of the valley alone. In 1897 authorities claimed to have uncovered Koʻolau's grave.

From the open ridge with its valley view the trail leads down through a grove of mango trees and crosses the main flow of Kalalau Stream. More terraces are visible beyond this crossing, and the trail to Waimakemake Falls, branches left among them. This turn-off is hard to find, even though in 1984 a troop of Boy Scouts worked hard to reestablish the trail after Hurricane Iwa closed it. Big Pool is only ten minutes from the last stream crossing. Here you can spend an entire day plunging into the cool water and sunning on the rocks wondering what the folks in New York City are doing.

2 SEEING NĀ PALI BY BOAT

The hike to Kalalau is 11 arduous miles on foot, but by boat the same destination is 6 miles sitting down. The Hawaiians were not lazy people, they simply never worked harder than they had to: which way do you think they preferred to travel to Kalalau? The valleys beyond Kalalau were accessible by trail from Kōke‘e in the Waimea district, but natives reserved the grueling 4,000-foot climb for the winter months when boat travel was too perilous.

Skimming along with a 100-horsepower engine snarling in your ears is a far cry from gliding with the swells in a canoe powered by muscle; yet the sweeping views, dramatic sea caves, and cavorting dolphins remain the same. For those venturing down the coast in kayaks or canoes the experience remains virtually the same as that of the Hawaiians in their outriggers.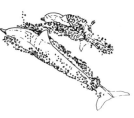

Exploring the coast by sea allows you to visit places not accessible by foot, and offers a panorama of spectacular scenery en route. Rugged individuals have swum the length of Nā Pali over the course of several days, others prefer the convenience of a ride in a 45-foot cabin cruiser for a few hours.

THE ROAD'S END

Your first sea view of the chiseled panorama of Nā Pali is offshore of Kē‘ē Beach, where the road ends.   #1

The Kalalau Trail starts here; the vertical slabs of basalt above the beach force a steep ascent of the trail, which soon disappears into the luxuriant growth.   #2

The Makana Cliffs tower 1,500 feet above the beach. During special celebrations Hawaiians hurled firebrands from the top of these cliffs for the entertainment of spectators below. This activity led to the nickname "Fireworks Cliff."   #3

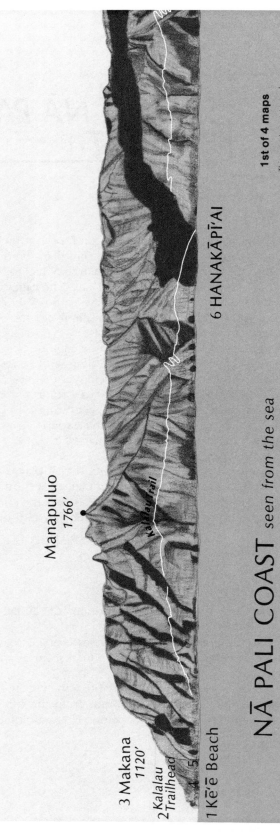

NĀ PALI COAST *seen from the sea*

3 Makana
1120'

2 Kalalau
Trailhead

1 Kē'ē Beach

4 5

Manapuluo
1766'

Kalalau Trail

6 HANAKĀPĪ'AI

From here the Allerton house is visible, although trees hide the road. #4
This house once belonged to Robert Allerton, a wealthy landscape designer from Illinois who moved to Kaua'i in 1937 (see page 1). The
house and grounds were used as a substitute for Queensland, Australia,
in filming a steamy love scene in the television miniseries "The Thorn-
birds."

A *hula hālau* and a *heiau* stand to the right of the house, looking #5
like a stack of terraces. Young Hawaiians were brought here to learn the
once-sacred hula dances, which have evolved into the dances now
seen in Waikiki's dance revues.

HANAKĀPĪ'AI

By boat you cover in five minutes what takes a hiker an hour to accom- #6
plish, arriving at Hanakāpī'ai Valley 1¼ miles past the beginning of the
cliffs at the road's end. Here tents nestle in the shadows of *hala* trees;
campers are allowed one night's stay on their way to Kalalau Valley. A
Hawaiian myth says that the valley was named after a Menehune
chiefess who died after giving birth. Literally, Hanakāpī'ai means "bay
sprinkling food," but you will recall that each Hawaiian word can have
several possible interpretations.

As the Hawaiians settled along the Nā Pali Coast they moved into
Hanakāpī'ai Valley first. Their thatched *hale,* or houses, dotted the valley floor where self-sufficient natives grew their staple food, taro, as
well as banana, sweet potato, sugar cane, and arrowroot. Taro was
grown in wet paddies, which also made convenient holding tanks for
edible freshwater shrimp and fish.

It is possible that as many as a few hundred Hawaiians made their
homes in Hanakāpī'ai Valley before the arrival of Westerners in 1778,
yet no written records exist to tell us the actual number. Coffee was
grown in Hanakāpī'ai Valley during the late nineteenth century, and a
coffee mill 1 mile inland processed the beans grown in the area. However, falling coffee prices and a lack of affordable labor led to the
demise of coffee cultivation on Kaua'i. By the end of the century there
were no people living in Hanakāpī'ai, although until 1903 natives commuted from nearby Hā'ena to grow taro.

The 4-mile, round-trip hike to Hanakāpī'ai takes half a day from the
road's end, and offers dramatic views, interesting plant life, and a
refreshing stream to bathe in. The gentle summer surf forms a pictur-
esque white sand beach at the mouth of the valley, but the digging
action of the powerful winter surf scoops the sand away, leaving only
rock rubble.

A strong, wind-driven current rips along the coast in the summer, making swimming risky; during the winter the pounding surf makes swimming extremely dangerous. Each year the list of drownings off the coast grows longer. Because of the large numbers of hikers using Hanakāpī'ai Beach, boat landings are prohibited.

HO'OLULU VALLEY AND SEA CAVE

#7   A lofty cliff forces hikers on the Kalalau Trail to ascend to an elevation of 800 feet before reaching Ho'olulu Valley (map point #8). The protected cove below this cliff might account for the valley's name, which means "protected bay or waters." Natives in their canoes took refuge in this cove and called it Pā Ma Wa'a, "the enclosure around canoes."

In the winter, massive waves hurl themselves against this *pali* (or cliff) and erupt into fans of spray as the backwash hits the next incoming swell. Over the eons this force has repeatedly undercut the cliff, and has caused the overhanging rock to collapse into the sea. The impressive wall of rock eighty stories high you see at Ho'olulu was caused by the force of the waves cutting farther and farther inland. Winter surf is still in the process of gouging out three more caves at the cliff's base.

Look above for the graceful seabirds, the *koa'e* (or white-tailed tropic birds), that nest in these cliffs.

Winter also brings the chance to view Hawai'i's magnificent marine mammal, the humpback whale. Leaving Alaska's frigid but bountiful waters in the late summer, approximately 40 humpbacks arrive in the waters off Kaua'i in time for Christmas to breed and bear their young. Nearly a year after mating, the female gives birth to her 2,000 pound offspring; this baby can grow into an adult weighing 40 tons and measuring 45 feet in length. By April hungry humpbacks head back north, having eaten little since reaching Hawai'i. The sight of a *koholā,* as the Hawaiians called these whales, throwing itself from the sea or simply flipping its powerful tail fluke renews one's admiration for the power and grace found in nature.

#9   Two miles down the coast a misty veil from the stream above drapes across Ho'olulu Sea Cave. On calm days boats enter this cave where Hawaiians once came to fish. Charcoal-colored marine birds called *noio* live in sea caves along the coast, tirelessly scolding all intruders who disrupt their tranquility. Streaks of their white droppings mark their perches in the rocky niches above. Their courting behavior of

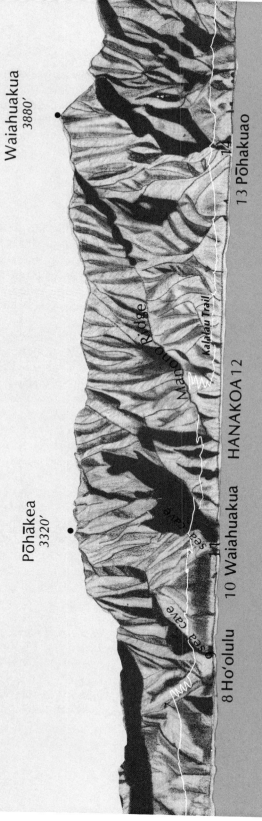

Waiahuakua
3880'

Pōhākea
3320'

Manono Ridge

Kalalau Trail

sea cave

sea cave

sea cave

8 Ho'olulu   10 Waiahuakua   HANAKOA 12   13 Pōhakuao

NĀ PALI COAST *seen from the sea*

2nd of 4 maps
This map is not to scale

nodding to one another earned them the nickname "noddy," which is used around the tropical Pacific and Atlantic oceans.

Rock terracing walls serve as evidence that the Hawaiians grew taro in Hoʻolulu Valley, although no house sites have been located in the area. It is possible, however, that natives lived in the neighboring valleys and commuted to Hoʻolulu to tend their crops.

WAIAHUAKUA VALLEY AND SEA CAVE

#10   Hikers travel 5 miles by trail to Waiahuakua Valley, but by sea it is only half as far. Waiahuakua is typical of valleys along the Nā Pali Coast, where rainfall runoff whittles down the lava slopes at the same time that the surf cuts away their seaward edges. As a result, these valleys have floors that sit well above sea level and so are called "hanging valleys." In Waiahuakua Valley the floor sits about 100 feet above sea level.

#11   One of the most startling sights along the coast greets you in Waiahuakua Sea Cave, where fresh water and sunlight gush into the inky darkness. Here erosion has worked its magic once again, cutting down the stream bed above while enlarging the sea cave below. What began as a slow seep of fresh water from above now floods through in a torrent.

Boat captains like to thrill their passengers by charging at full throttle into the dark recesses of the cave, making a quick turn at the last second, then darting out a back entrance that leads safely to sea. A tale recounts how a Hawaiian fisherman took advantage of the cave's back entrance to evade some oceangoing robbers. Six men in a canoe gave chase to this fishermen who was returning to Hāʻena with a boatload of fish. Seeking refuge in the westernmost cave, he quietly paddled around and out the other entrance, while his pursuers, ignorant of the cave's second entrance, waited patiently for him to reappear.

HANAKOA VALLEY

#12   Halfway to Kalalau, Hanakoa Valley makes a convenient overnight stop for hikers. A series of cascades courses down the 2,000-foot-high cliff behind Hanakoa. The translation of the name Hanakoa is ambiguous, meaning either "bay of the koa tree" or "bay of the warriors."

The physical formation and cultural history of Hanakoa are almost identical to the last valley you passed, Waiahuakua. Archaeological remains indicate that Hanakoa once cradled a sizable Hawaiian farming community. Fifty Hawaiians lived in this valley in 1835, but by the late 1800s they had abandoned taro farming and modified the terraces for growing coffee trees.

Passing Hanakoa on a calm day, try to imagine sacks of cured coffee beans being tossed from the rock ledge into open boats below. Offshore a larger ship would lie at anchor, waiting to load the coffee cargo. The coffee growers also loaded the sacks onto mules or horses that picked their way 6 miles out on the Kalalau Trail.

Ocean currents often converge off Manono Ridge where the coast curves slightly southward. A current that pushes paddlers from Kēʻē Beach may switch direction, making it a struggle to get to Kalalau. Although the current runs from Kēʻē to Kalalau as long as the tradewinds blow, my experience shows that the current reverses direction once the wind lightens.

PŌHAKUAO

The path to Kalalau becomes quite obvious past Hanakoa, where the vegetation thins out. Just around the corner from Hanakoa the trail dips down to within 200 feet above sea level—the lowest point since Hanakāpīʻai Beach. Often you can see hikers teetering along this narrow section of trail. #13

Notice how the combination of lighter rainfall, drying wind, winter sea spray, and the increasing number of goats has prevented anything except brush and grass from growing on the ridges beyond Hanakoa. Because plant life is relatively less luxuriant west of Hanakoa, erosion gains the upper hand in areas where goats and landslides strip the vegetation from the earth. Large valleys give way to numerous small gullies along this section of the coastline.

The area between Hanakoa and Kalalau once made up an ancient Hawaiian land division named Pōhakuao. Pōhakuao was the smallest of five such land divisions, or *ahupuaʻa,* along the Nā Pali Coast. Natives living in Pōhakuao grew the hemplike *olonā* plant for making fishnets and cordage; later it was harvested for commercial use. The Hawaiians also cultivated taro on the level areas in the middle of the Pōhakuao division.

Four miles by boat from Kēʻē Beach, the ocean has worn an arch through the weathered basaltic rock. In calm seas small craft can safely fit through this opening. #14

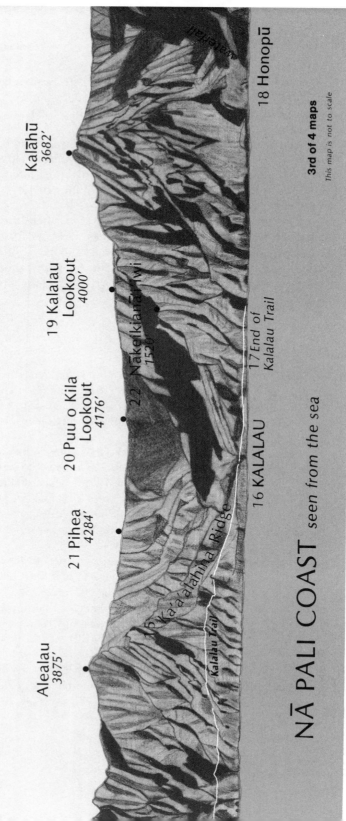

Alealau
3875'

Kalāhū
3682'

21 Pihea
4284'

20 Puu o Kila
Lookout
4176'

19 Kalalau
Lookout
4000'

22 Nākeikianā'iwi
1520'

15 Ka'a'alahina Ridge

Kalalau Trail

16 KALALAU

17 End of
Kalalau Trail

waterfall

18 Honopū

NĀ PALI COAST *seen from the sea*

3rd of 4 maps

This map is not to scale

KALALAU

Kalalau Valley

Kalalau Valley, the largest valley on the Nā Pali Coast, spreads 2 miles   #16
wide and reaches 2 miles inland. Enclosed by 4,000-foot-high cliffs,
Kalalau has an extensive complex of archaeologial sites in addition to
its waterfalls and pools, wild fruit, and excellent camping.

    The trail enters Kalalau Valley at Kaʻaʻalahina Ridge. When they
reach this point sweaty hikers have traveled 4 miles more on the winding trail than is covered to the same destination by boat. The trail leads
2 more miles to Kalalau Beach, beyond which travel along the coast by
land is impossible.

    Native-built terracing covers every usable acre of Kalalau Valley,
indicating that a sizable population lived there before Westerners discovered Hawaiʻi. Two hundred people made their home in the *ahupuaʻa* of Kalalau in 1847; their *hale* were scattered among the taro paddies.

    Some inhabitants exported taro by canoe from Kalalau to Hanalei,
where they traded their crop for other staples. Others made a liquor
called *ōkolehao* from the root of the *ti* plant, then carried it up the
4,000-foot cliff to Kōkeʻe to trade. After the last Hawaiian family
moved out in 1919 cattle grazed in the Kalalau *ahupuaʻa.*

    In June of 1893 Deputy Sheriff Louis Stolz of Waimea attempted to
round up and deport a group of eight lepers who were hiding in Kalalau. But on the evening of June 27, Stolz lay dead, shot by Koʻolau, a
leper who had fled with his son and wife to Kalalau from Waimea.

    Eighty police and soldiers, whose arms included a howitzer, failed to
capture Koʻolau and his family. They remained in hiding for two years
until the death of Koʻolau and his son. Koʻolau's wife hiked up out of
the valley alone to return to her family near Waimea. In 1897 authorities claimed to have finally uncovered Koʻolau's grave in Kalalau.

Kalalau Beach

Depending on annual variations in the surging surf, Kalalau Beach   #17
varies from a thin ribbon of sand 100 yards long to a sandy swath that
extends to the westernmost of several caves that lie at the end of the
beach. Colorful tents dot the flat spaces above the sand, and when the
summer surf enlarges the beach, campers move into the nearby caves
as well. The state issues permits for up to five nights of camping in the
area.

Behind the beach Hoʻoleʻa Falls provides drinking water, showering facilities, and an idyllic backdrop for campers. The beach is usually at its greatest length in August; at this time hikers are able to walk down to the large rockslide at the west end. Two caves here collapsed in the spring of 1987, leaving a pile of huge boulders where campers once pitched their tents. On calm days you can see people swimming to and from the next valley, Honopū (map point #18). However, a strong current runs out to sea from this point—it carries its share of people to their final resting place.

The state allows private boats with permits to land at Kalalau Beach, yet only a few commercial companies have permits to bring passengers ashore. Zooming ashore in a motor-powered inflatable boat requires skill—the captain must dash in between waves and yank up the outboard engines the instant the boat hisses up onto the sand. Moreover, getting dropped off by boat is no guarantee that Mother Nature will let you leave by boat; because the surf can rise quickly boaters may be forced either to wait or to hike 11 miles to civilization. Many visitors ride the 6 miles in by boat, stay a few nights, then hike out with a relatively light pack.

From the ocean two notches are visible along the forested ridgeline behind Kalalau Valley. These lookouts on Kalalau's 4,000-foot rim offer another stunning perspective—knife-edge ridges flank the valley like draped green velvet folding down toward the sea.

#19   At Kalalau Lookout, 8 miles beyond Waimea Canyon Lookout, the view includes Waimakemake Falls (where Koʻolau hid) as well as the blue ocean contrasting against the red hues of Kaʻaʻalahina Ridge.

#20   The paved road ends 1 mile farther at Puu o Kila, but the remnants of an unsuccessful road project continue as a wide trail to Pihea peak (map point #21) just over a mile hike to the east. From this trail Kalalau Beach is visible, although the falls lie hidden by intervening ridges.

HONOPŪ

#18   Honopū offers one of the most enchanting settings along the Nā Pali Coast: two wide sand beaches divided by a dramatic arch and flanked by a small waterfall. Above, the valley walls rise in a stunning array of knife edges—to which a friend jokingly refers as "the corduroy effect." Hollywood invaded these beaches to film the 1976 remake of *King Kong,* in which Jessica Lange bathes at the falls, and for which special-effects wizards built an "imaginary" wall to contain the giant ape.

In 1922 a party of adventurers who camped at Honopū reported see-

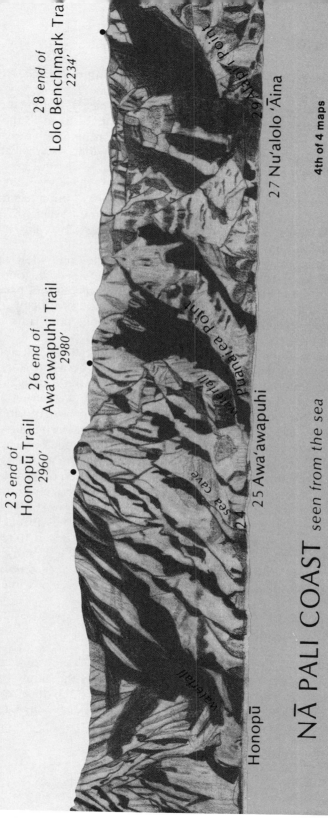

23 end of
Honopū Trail
2960'

26 end of
Awa'awapuhi Trail
2980'

28 end of
Lolo Benchmark Trail
2234'

27 Nu'alolo 'Āina

26 'Alapi'i Point

Honopū

waterfall

sea cave

waterfall

Punaiea Point

24

25 Awa'awapuhi

NĀ PALI COAST *seen from the sea*

4th of 4 maps

This map is not to scale

ing a fishing shrine nestled in the dunes behind the beach. However, this monument has not been seen since that time.

The valley floor stands 150 feet above the beach, making it difficult to view. Archaeologists are doubtful that natives lived in the valley; Honopū's narrowness left little level land for farming, and nearby Kalalau offered much better conditions for growing taro. Probably few farmers bothered to clamber up over the arch to cultivate crops in Honopū.

The best translation of Honopū is "conch bay," but a legend about the mythical Mū people gives it the nickname "Valley of the Lost Tribe." Recent accidents involving people trying to hike into the valley serve as a warning to intrepid explorers today.

Like Honopū, the coastline beyond this valley offers few sites suitable for growing crops. An ancient trail once connected Honopū with Nuʻalolo ʻĀina farther down the coast, but the 2,500-foot battlements above and the 100-foot sea cliffs below made access difficult. The state maintained a trail above Honopū's western ridge until Hurricane Iwa buried it under debris in 1982 (map point #23).

#24   Three-quarters of a mile beyond Honopū the Open-ceiling Cave offers the only protection for boats traveling between Honopū and Nuʻalolo. Entering through the dark arch with the backlight glowing through the turquoise water gives the feeling of entering a natural cathedral. My father delighted in first showing my husband and me this cave by having us face toward the rear of the boat as he piloted us in. Unable to see ahead we thought we were entering another dark sea cave, but what a surprise we had as we burst into the sunlit interior.

Hawaiians must have rested in this natural haven on canoe trips up the coast; I wonder what legends they told to describe its unusual formation. Did their volcano goddess, Pele, dig it? It is sad that today we do not even know what the Hawaiians called it. A few fish find refuge in the cave's collapsed roof, but the barren sand bottom 30 feet below is a marine desert. The walls of the cave do host a wealth of sealife, however; possibly the Hawaiians came here to collect *ʻopihi,* the limpet whose wrinkled shell protects it from the scourge of winter's surf.

AWAʻAWAPUHI

#25   A quarter-mile farther, mysterious Awaʻawapuhi Valley curves inland— arcing around out of sight; from the ocean only the mouth of this valley is visible. The sun seldom shines into this 3,000-foot-deep chasm that has been gouged out by 6 million years of rain. One legend explains the serpentine shape of this valley: a huge *puhi,* or eel, slithered up onto this slope and left the indentation of his body before the lava had solidified.

This valley astounded me when I first followed its gurgling brook back 1 mile to the valley head and found the falls dry. Downhill from the falls, a hanging garden of watercress and maidenhair fern (see page 21) reveal a series of springs that feed the stream during the dry summer months.

Descendents of the first goats brought by Captain George Vancouver in the 1790s keep the valley floor cleared of large plants, leaving only air plant and lantana. The wild ginger *'awapuhi,* from which the valley gets its name, no longer thrives there.

Above the beach 150 feet you can see a horizontal ledge in the sea cliff where Hawaiians inched their way along to Honopū. To the right a waterfall floods into the sea, blocking entry for people as well as the stream creatures that return to the sea as part of their life cycles. The scarcity of stream life and lack of level land for farming limited the number of natives who lived in Awa'awapuhi.

A well-preserved *heiau* sits at the base of the cliffs on the east bank of Awa'awapuhi Stream—another stands on Puanaiea Point to your right. Look closely to see the edge of the rock platforms where Hawaiians came to make offerings and prayers.

Hawaiians gained entry to Awa'awapuhi Valley over the serrated ridges that separate it from Nu'alolo 'Āina to the southwest. It is possible that they also climbed up from below when calm seas allowed canoes to land on the beach. Entry into the valley is extremely perilous and so is discouraged by the state.

I recommend the Awa'awapuhi Trail for those with an insatiable   #26
curiosity and a love for arduous uphill hikes. This trail begins at an elevation of 4,000 feet in Kōke'e, 1 mile beyond the Kōke'e Museum. In 3¼ miles it drops over 1,000 feet to a knife-edge ridge with dizzying views of Awa'awapuhi Valley on one side and Nu'alolo Valley on the other. A sheer drop of 3,000 feet makes it impossible to hike into the valleys below, and people have fallen to their deaths after having lost their footing while simply looking over the edge of this drop. The return hike puts your heart and sweat glands to work as you gain back the altitude that you spent going down—the price to be paid for a memorable view.

NUʻALOLO ʻĀINA

#27   Like Awaʻawapuhi, Nuʻalolo Valley reveals few of its hidden treasures to boat viewers, although hikers can peer into it from the trail above. Nuʻalolo ʻĀina was described by one archaeologist as the most impressive of the Nā Pali valleys; its broad valley floor accommodates a complex network of native-built terrace walls while the surrounding cliffs are pockmarked with ancient burial caves.

There are two areas along the coast called Nuʻalolo, which is a name with no translated meaning. To differentiate between the two places the Hawaiians called one Nuʻalolo Kai, indicating its location by the sea *(kai),* and called the other *ʻāina,* meaning land. A cliff separates the two areas, and so natives fashioned a ladder from two coconut trees to allow travel between the two settlements. The ladder was located at Alapiʻi Point (map point #29); *alapiʻi* means "ascent" in Hawaiian. Together the two communities in Nuʻalolo were self-sufficient—food crops were grown in Nuʻalolo ʻĀina while neighboring Nuʻalolo Kai supplied all of the necessary seafood.

A group of adventurers traveled the land route between the two areas in 1922. Landing in Nuʻalolo Kai, they climbed into Nuʻalolo ʻĀina to hunt for goats and explore. In one cave they found a canoe in which human bones and artifacts had been interred—a common burial practice for high-ranking Hawaiians. Unfortunately, they dislodged the canoe with its sacred cargo and sent it crashing to the valley floor.

After the last natives left Nuʻalolo ʻĀina around 1900, the ladder connecting Nuʻalolo ʻĀina with Nuʻalolo Kai disintegrated and the Kamaile Trail from Kōkeʻe washed away, thus cutting off access and leaving the valley in peaceful repose. In 1984 a hiker fell to his death when he slipped from the grassy bluff onto the boulder beach 75 feet below. Entry into Nuʻalolo ʻĀina is dangerous and is not encouraged.

As you skirt around the wide reef that shelters Nuʻalolo Kai, look for turtles bobbing on the sea's surface; the dark shells of these cold-blooded creatures assist in soaking up the sun. Turtles can go for hours without air while dozing, but otherwise they must lift their heads to breathe every few minutes. Unlike the intelligent dolphins and whales who also need to breathe air, turtles rival pigeons for brains. The

Ladder leading from Nuʻalolo Kai to Nuʻalolo ʻĀina. (From Bishop Museum photo collection)

hawksbill and green sea turtle found along
this coast are both endangered species pro-
tected by law. The Hawaiians called all turtles
honu. Natives captured turtles with nets or
spears and men ate the flesh—women were
not allowed to eat turtle meat. The Hawaiians
carved fishhooks, combs, and scraping tools from turtle shell.

Before heading into the bay at Nuʻalolo Kai look for the small island
of Niʻihau on the western horizon. Niʻihau is privately owned by a
local *haole* family who bought it for ten thousand dollars from Kamehameha V in 1864. A great deal of mystique surrounds this dry island
where ranching is the main endeavor. Erroneous rumors abound claim-
ing that Niʻihau's 250 residents are all full-blooded Hawaiians. It is,
however, the last island in Hawaiʻi where Hawaiian is still spoken as the
principal language.

NUʻALOLO KAI

Imposing cliffs encircle the beach at Nuʻalolo Kai, which is 9 miles
from Kēʻē Beach. These cliffs bear Pele's volcanic signature: two dikes
slashed in the form of an X. As you enter the protection of the reef,
Kamaile Peak towers 1,300 feet above you. Named for the fragrant
maile vine, Hawaiian fishermen returning home at night steered
toward the silhouette of this knob to guide their canoes safely through
the jagged coral.

These sheer cliffs offered a perfect site for the Hawaiian firework displays, *ʻōahi*. The audience perched in canoes offshore, watching as
burning bits of wood thrown from above sparkled and danced on the
updrafts. Even King Kamehameha III came to Nuʻalolo to view this
spectacular nighttime display. You might recall that natives also had
firefalls off Makana Cliffs at Kēʻē Beach.

The reef-sheltered cove at Nuʻalolo Kai offers the only reliably safe
landing along the entire coast, so natives used it as a way station when
canoeing between Hanalei to the north and Waimea to the south. Even
travelers bound for the island of Niʻihau would depart from Nuʻalolo Kai.

The first Westerner to land at Nuʻalolo Kai was Hiram Bingham, a
Protestant missionary. During his visit in 1822 he counted 70 natives
fishing in the cove, indicating that at least 100 people lived in the area.
In 1845 another visitor described the community as "a few miserable
huts."

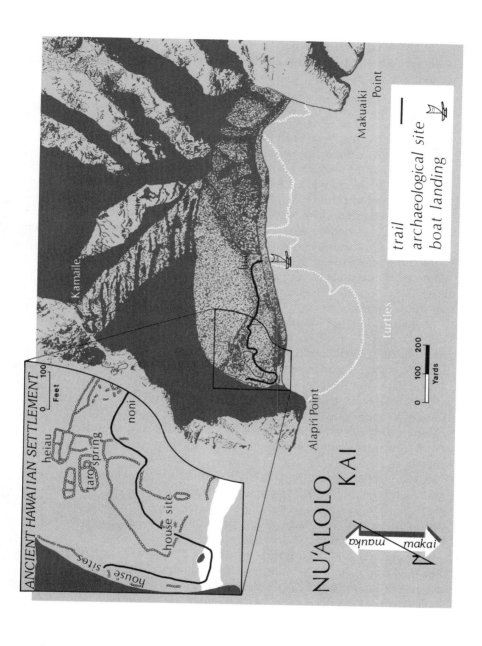

ANCIENT HAWAIIAN SETTLEMENT

heiau

taro spring

noni

house site

house sites

0   100
Feet

Kamaile

Makuaiki
Point

turtles

Alapiʻi Point

NUʻALOLO
KAI

mauka

makai

trail
archaeological site
boat landing

0   100   200
Yards

Today private boats need no permit to land at Nuʻalolo Kai, yet only a limited number of commercial boats have landing permits. The state does not allow overnight camping at this beach.

The Reef

Imagine that you arrived with Bingham. Under the stillness of the cliffs the sound of women fishing along the coral apron drifts out to greet you. They banter back and forth as they bend to pick edible *limu* (seaweed), shellfish, crabs, and fish, which they tuck into calabashes that bob along behind them. Children dawdle nearby, occasionally shrieking with pain and delight as they catch crabs that they quickly dismember to eat. The men departed at dawn, steering their canoes toward a cloud of birds—an indication of a school of fish.

Floating along the edge of the coral reef with a diving mask gives a glimpse of the abundance of sea life that once sustained the area's inhabitants. Locals still come to Nuʻalolo Kai to set nets and pole fish for their dinners.

Undaunted by the scouring winter swell, tiny coral polyps gradually built the reef by secreting layer upon layer of calcium. At night these creatures hang out fan-like nets to filter food from the ocean water, but during the day they shrink back into the pores in the coral. Look closely at a piece of coral—its surface is pockmarked with entrances to these polyp condominiums. Only the outer $1/16$ inch of the coral is alive, building on the layers of abandoned calcium beneath. Calcium-bearing plants also help to cement this reef together.

Many people expect more brilliant colors than the subtle patches of yellow, pink, and blue that they see in Hawaiʻi's reefs. Polyps give coral its color, so once taken out of the water coral fades along with the life of the animals within. The parrotfish, or *uhu*, feeds on coral polyps; it grinds up the coral with its powerful parrot-like beak then eliminates the ground-up calcium. Thus sand is formed as a by-product of parrotfish feeding activity.

On the reef's surface large, black sluglike sea cucumbers (a), or *loli*, inch their way across the coral along with the spiny sea urchins *(wana)* (b)—the sea's answer to the porcupine. The Hawaiians believed that *wana* were one of the forms taken by the spirits of their ancestors. These *ʻaumakua* acted as guardian spirits, and in return natives took special care of whatever entity they considered to be their family *ʻaumakua*. Spirits might also take the form of the delicious *heʻe* (octo-

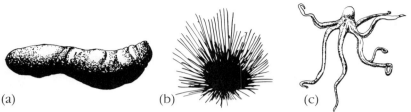

(a)   (b)   (c)

pus) (c) or *honu* found around the reef. Fishermen today still scour this reef for *he'e* and consider them a prize for supper.

Larger fish live along the edge of the coral where deeper water and coral ledges offer better hunting and refuge. Look for the 1- to 2-foot-long dusky green fish, *kala,* whose protruding  forehead won it the nickname "unicornfish." The Hawaiians kept time for their chants and hulas with small coconut shell drums covered with the tough skin of *kala* fish.

The Hawaiian names for many seaweeds and fish reflect the interrelationship of the land and sea. Seaweeds share names with plants growing ashore, while some fish are named for leaves and birds. The name of a round, yellow butterflyfish, *lauhau* (d), means "leaf of the hau,"

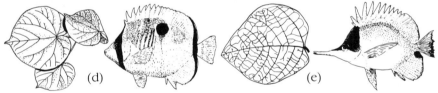

(d)   (e)

because it resembles that leaf in shape. Another brilliant yellow butterflyfish, the *lauwiliwili,* gets its name from the leaves *(lau)* of the *wiliwili* tree, which sheds its leaves in a rain of yellow. (These trees still grow on the south side of Kaua'i's main harbor, appropriately called Nāwiliwili.) The name of one variety of this fish, the *lauwiliwili nukunuku 'oi'oi* (e), rivals for length that of the famous *humuhumunukunukuāpua'a.*

Members of the wrasse family abound along the reef fringe: species commonly seen include the ornate and Christmas wrasses in their vibrant pinks and blues, and the more subdued blue and green saddle wrasse that wears orange  "saddles." The Hawaiians made religious offerings to various deities of this popular family of fish called *hīnālea,* and also ate them raw or charcoal broiled. According to legend, *hīnālea* sprang from the remains of two supernatural beings who were torn asunder by an angry goddess.

Anyone who eats fish taken from waters off Nā Pali risks becoming ill from ingesting a toxic microorganism called ciguatera. Cooking the fish makes no difference; if the fish has fed on algae that contains the ciguatera organisms, eating it produces vomiting, weakness, numbness, and shock. Recent cases have been traced to one type of algae-eating fish, but even carnivorous fish that have eaten these algae eaters can pass on the toxin. Be safe and leave the fish for sightseeing. The Hawaii State Department of Health can give you more information about ciguatera poisoning.

The Hawaiian Settlement

By restricting the number of boats that land at Nuʻalolo Kai, the Division of State Parks hopes to preserve the area's archaeological sites and keep the bay from being overwhelmed with people. If you are lucky enough to be allowed ashore here, take a walk down the beach to the east.

A bush with bright green, succulent leaves grows behind the beach at Nuʻalolo Kai. Snorkelers outside the state park crush these *naupaka* leaves and rub them inside their face masks to prevent condensation from forming. The ½-inch-wide white flowers of the *naupaka* bush appear to be torn in half, and thus have inspired numerous legends. 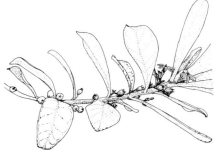 One myth explains how a Hawaiian woman ripped these flowers in half after a lovers' spat, refusing to forgive her lover until he brought her a whole flower. Needless to say he died bereft, unable to appease her. There are other legends about the *naupaka,* one of which is described on page 17.

The buoyant white seeds of the *naupaka* floated across the Pacific to Hawaiʻi's shores. Water stored in its fuzzy, succulent leaves allows the *naupaka* to thrive on Hawaiʻi's driest shorelines.

Farther east, walk inland from a stand of ironwood trees to the large rock platform hidden by the thick brush. Here priests, or *kahuna,* once performed rituals and left offerings of different foods to ensure successful crops. An agricultural *heiau,* called a *hoʻoulu ʻai,* like this one honored the god Lono.

Every year between October and February, the Hawaiians honored Lono during a four-month period of thanksgiving called the Makahiki. After paying the annual tribute to their chiefs, the Hawaiians celebrated, feasted, and played games. During this period war was *kapu.*

Part of the reason that the Hawaiians mistook Captain Cook for Lono was that his arrival in Hawaiʻi coincided with the Makahiki. Nowadays Hawaiians still leave symbolic offerings of a stone wrapped in a *ti* leaf at Lono's *hoʻoulu ʻai*. For the sake of the *ti* plants, however, please do not imitate this practice.

The Hawaiians worshipped four major deities: Kāne, creator of all living things; Kanaloa, god of the wind and sea; Kū, the god of war; and Lono, the god of harvest. The missionaries totally baffled the Hawaiians by telling them that worshipping four deities was pagan, yet at the same time urging them to accept the Christian trinity of the Father, Son, and Holy Spirit.

A freshwater spring east of the *heiau* supplied the inhabitants of Nuʻalolo Kai with drinking water made brackish by sea water seeping into the low-lying pool. Taro sometimes grows here—it is easy to identify its heart-shaped leaves. The former inhabitants of the area cultivated sweet potatoes, a hardy vine well-suited to the dry coastal conditions of Nuʻalolo Kai. Look for the 2-foot-long glossy leaves of the *ti* plant (see page 11) as well as *noni* (a), an interesting Polynesian introduction that grows nearby (see page 42).

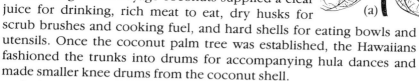

(a)

Coconut palms are also a prominant feature in the area. The well-packaged nuts from this tree can sprout even after falling 60 feet or floating in the ocean for three months. In spite of the durability of the nut, scholars believe that the all-purpose coconut palm first came to Hawaiʻi with Polynesian settlers. On the long canoe voyage coconuts supplied a clear juice for drinking, rich meat to eat, dry husks for scrub brushes and cooking fuel, and hard shells for eating bowls and utensils. Once the coconut palm tree was established, the Hawaiians fashioned the trunks into drums for accompanying hula dances and made smaller knee drums from the coconut shell.

Green coconuts often fall victim to hungry rats who savor the meat then set up housekeeping in the hollowed-out shell. I once found a rat's nest complete with a lining of facial tissue and photographic film. The meat inside a brown nut is good to eat if the nut sloshes when shaken—although the brown color also indicates that the juice has fermented.

Returning to the beach, turn right and walk to the base of the cliff.

The old trail to Nu'alolo 'Āina started on the ledge to your left. During calm summer weather this is a great spot for turtle watching, and the fishing pole holders cemented in the rocks here indicate that the area is also favored by fishermen.

Following the cliff inland you pass a series of eight platforms snuggled under the overhanging cliff protected from the wind and rain. These platforms were the foundation for Hawaiian *hale* during the settlement of the area. Archaeologists have unearthed remnants of grass thatching, calabashes, seashells, and fishhooks dated around A.D. 1380 at these sites.

A typical *hale* was thatched with grass and had only one opening, a low door. Before Westerners brought metal nails, the wood framework of poles on which thatching hung had to be lashed together.

The *hale* consisted of a single room lit by the dim flicker of a string of oily *kukui* nut kernels. The dirt floor of the room was generally covered with mats woven from *lau hala*. The estate of a *konohiki* (page 33) included up to five buildings for sleeping and working, with separate eating huts for the men and women. Commoners, however, made do with one hut, which was used mostly for sleeping. Only during rain storms or at times of *kapu* when their religious practices dictated that they stay indoors, did the Hawaiians seek refuge in their *hale*.

(a)

Normally the women sat out in the shade of *milo* (a) trees to pound paper mulberry bark into *tapa* cloth; there they were joined by the old men who braided sennit, a coconut fiber rope. Sennit lashings held together the framework of a *hale* and secured outriggers to Hawaiian canoes.

MILOLI'I

The beach at Miloli'i is a mile farther along the coast—it lies just around Makuaiki Point at the western end of Nu'alolo Kai. The name is derived from the Hawaiian word for the "fine twist" of a fiber rope made from coconut fibers or perhaps from the inner bark of the *milo* tree. Unlike the two places named Nu'alolo, Miloli'i's beach and valley join together; thus the Hawaiians who once lived there were provided with a sheltered valley for taro farming, a reef for fishing, and a beach for launching canoes.

Above a rubble bluff at the east end of Miloli'i, freshwater springs seep out over a layer of dense lava, tinging the dry cliff face with

trail
campground
boat landing
shelter
archaeological site

MILOLI'I

MILOLI'I Ridge

Anaki Ridge

Pa'aiki Falls

MILOLI'I VALLEY

Miloli'i Stream

falls

water tank

heiau

MILOLI'I BEACH

Keawanui

Makuaiki Point

mauka   makai

0   100   200   Yards

patches of green. Parched by the neverending sun and wind, the 1,400-foot-high cliffs at Miloliʻi stand in arid contrast to the verdant *pali* on the east side of the Nā Pali Coast. The clouds that bathe Hanakāpīʻai in 75 inches of rain every year sprinkle less than 20 inches of rain annually onto Miloliʻi.

Below the bluff the shoreline is skirted by a fringing reef that breaks slightly by the sand beach, allowing small boats to land in the summer. This small channel was blasted in the early 1950s by the territorial government, which also built three shelters, a cabin (now used by State Parks personnel), a *lua,* and showers. On sunny summer days these showers run hot; the piped-in water is warmed by the sun as it travels from its source in the valley beyond. Another advantage is offered by the ironwood trees, which were planted in the 1960s to provide some shelter from the afternoon winds. The hot showers, as well as the running water and shelters, make Miloliʻi the most luxurious of the campgrounds on the coast. Camping stays here are restricted to three days per month.

Miloliʻi's History

Archaeologists estimate that perhaps 50 families lived along the coastal flat behind Miloliʻi Beach, and more natives are estimated to have lived in *hale* and cave shelters located in the valley. A *heiau* measuring 200 feet by 90 feet stood on the bluff east of the campsites; another is believed to have stood where a mound is now seen west of the cabin. Inhabitants secreted the bones of their kin in the formidable cliffs surrounding the beach and valley.

Native life at Miloliʻi paralleled that at Nuʻalolo, although farming was not as productive. In the shade of *milo* trees women sat working paper mulberry bark into *tapa,* while men repaired their fishnets. Inland, men tended to the taro patches as women and children hunted for edible *ʻōpae* (shrimp), *ʻoʻopu* (goby fish), and *hīhīwai* (mollusks) along the stream bed. Until the arrival of Westerners this valley and beach provided the Hawaiians with everything they needed.

Western education came to Miloliʻi in the form of a school that was constructed on the raised valley floor above the boulder beach, just south of the stream and above the existing remains of a *heiau.* During the 1870s the teacher, Kanuikino, hiked 6 miles every day from his home in Mana to instruct his 30 or so pupils. By the turn of the century, however, only four families remained in the region: gradually the lure of opportunity drew many of Miloiʻi's residents away and foreign diseases made inroads into the native population.

Grass huts at Miloli'i, circa 1890. (From Bishop Museum photo collection)

In the 1950s an airstrip was constructed along the coast where taro had once been grown in terraces, between the stream and the government-owned cabin. The airstrip was constructed for biplanes that transported fishermen and artifact hunters visiting the area. At that time one house still stood near the school site.

The Beach

The winter surf bestows a wealth of shells on Miloli'i Beach, which makes it a favorite shell-hunting ground for locals and tour boat operators. Cone shells (a) and ruffled white cowries (b)

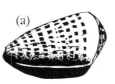

are common among the treasures cast upon this shore. The Hawaiians made lures to catch *he'e* from certain cowries, while in Tonga white cowries were placed above doorways to signify that a person of high rank lived within.

Miloli'i is one of the few beaches in Hawai'i where you can find the miniscule *momi* shells used in making Ni'ihau shell leis. Most of these highly prized necklaces come from the island of Ni'ihau, where these shells and the time needed to string them are both plentiful. The tremendous value of these leis comes from the hours of labor incurred in collecting the shells, hand drilling infinitesimal *puka*s (holes) in them, and then stringing the carefully sorted shells into decorative patterns.

Examples of this fine workmanship and their accompanying price tags can be seen at the Kaua'i Museum as well as in jewelry stores around the island.

In 1982 my husband and my father nearly stumbled over another rarity—a Hawaiian monk seal that had hefted its weight up onto this beach for a rest. Only two native mammals, the hoary bat and the monk seal, found their way to Hawai'i's shores, while other mammals, unable to fly or swim, depended on man to provide them with transportation. It was also man who hunted Hawai'i's monk seals and their Mediterranean cousins to the verge of extinction earlier in this century. Now the 500 remaining Hawaiian monk seals, one of only two types of tropical seals in the world, live in the chain of atolls northwest of Kaua'i under the protection of the U.S. Fish and Wildlife Service.

Low tide allows you to walk on the reef east of the sand beach, offering an interesting view of this coral kingdom. The same sea creatures that live at Nu'alolo Kai inhabit this reef. We found an excellent place for fishing at Makuaiki Point; however, it is accessible only by clinging to a narrow ledge that is exposed only during the lowest tide. (*Caution:* This is dangerous during any swell.) Here we fish for *hīnālea*, watch sea turtles basking on the surface, and take in the expansive view of Miloli'i.

In the calm of morning, acrobatic dolphins often greet campers at Miloli'i. Once on an early morning paddle from Miloli'i to Nu'alolo a dolphin catapulted out of the sea between our kayaks. They seem to enjoy loafing in the serene sea and are more difficut to spot as the afternoon wind roils the ocean's surface.

Evenings at Miloli'i begin with sunsets dappled by the few clouds that survived their journey along the coast. These clouds parade along the horizon like a lineup of animals, coaxing the imagination to play.

With the right conditions you can see the green flash, a phenomenon that is caused by light bending through the Earth's atmosphere. For the flash to occur, the last bit of sun must set directly into the sea, not into a bank of clouds. An overly enthusiastic viewer named this phenomenon, so do not expect a flash of green light to burst forth as the last bit of sun melts into the sea. Instead, keep track of the sun's progress with occasional glimpses, and protect your eyes from being flooded with light. As the last sliver of sun disappears, watch for an emerald hue that appears for a few seconds. That is it. Anticlimatic? Perhaps, but you can count yourself among the few who have seen the green flash, an honor that will win you points with the regulars at Tahiti Nui restaurant in Hanalei.

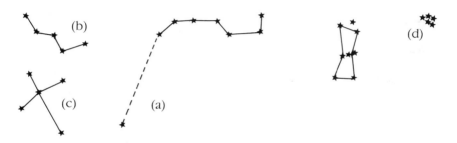

Far from city lights, nightfall at Miloli'i begins a spectacular planetar-ium show that is seldom obscured by clouds. The cliffs block the southerly constellations, but the Big Dipper (a), Cassiopeia (b), Cygnus (c), and the Pleiades (d), in addition to the cast of the zodiac, entertain throughout the night.

In the summer months the braying of a native seabird, the *'a'o,* serenades campers. Unfortunately you often see their pathetic, limp, black-and-white carcasses on the road when driving around the island. Coming into shore to nest after a day of fish-ing the *'a'o* are hypnotized by headlights and streetlights and lured to their untimely death. For-tunately Miloli'i offers no such dangers and for an hour at dusk their raspy call echoes off the cliffs as they wing their way inland to their mountain nests hidden in *uluhe* fern.

Miloli'i Valley

Miloli'i Valley is only 1 mile long, so the trail that leads up it is an easy walk from camp. The trail starts near the water tank above the west end of the flat. You have passed the turnoff if you end up at the stream mouth. Miloli'i is technically a hanging valley—as you can see from the 60-foot climb to reach the valley floor—yet it is not as spectacular as those you passed on your way down the coast.

Through the *koa haole* overgrowth you can still see an extensive tier of terracing walls that extend ¼ mile inland. Here Hawaiians raised taro, but farther inland the valley is too dry and too narrow to farm. A water pipe leading to an intake follows the path, below which maidenhair ferns adorn a waterfall barely tall enough to stand under. A rock behind the cascade makes a comfortable seat as the pummeling water massages your neck and back. Sitting under the falls and looking up under the boulders over which the water tumbles, you might see black cap-shaped *hīhīwai,* a type of mollusk favored as a food source by the Hawaiians.

Kukui trees, one of the last vestiges of the native Hawaiian plant life of the valley, shade the walk inland. Wild taro still persists in patches along the stream and introduced Java plum trees bow over the trail. I have even seen blackberries, whose seeds washed down from where the plant has been established in Kōke'e, trying to grasp a thorny stronghold in a cool, moist, patch of shade. Is it inevitable that this scourge of the cooler environs above will eventually adapt to warm coastal conditions? Let us hope it will take thousands of years for blackberries to adapt completely, thereby making this valley trail impassable.

Miloli'i Stream forks halfway up the valley: to the right (south) Pa'aiki Falls runs during heavy rains, while the main branch continues on to a larger waterfall. The main falls is above an unassuming pool and 8-foot-high falls. During dry spells springs trickle from the walls of the small pool, although most of this fork of Miloli'i Stream is fed by a source in Kōke'e above. Climbing above this point is not recommended—footing is virtually nonexistent. If you risk following the stream around the corner a narrow chasm gives you the feeling of being in some branch of the Grand Canyon. Around the next corner the bare cliffs dwarf you as you clamber up a small hill where a waterfall 100 feet high tumbles down the naked rock face.

Silt, loosened by feral goats that graze on the slopes above, chokes the stream and taints the plunge pool below the falls. The old Hawaiian trail that once traversed down 1,800 feet from Kōke'e into Miloli'i has likewise fallen victim to erosion and should not be attempted.

You might pass a goat carcass on your valley walk because the area is still open to goat hunting. The season starts in the first full week of August, and for eight weeks the Division of Forestry and Wildlife allows hunting on weekends. Hunters need a permit to shoot their one-goat allowance every season.

Some enterprising soul even tried to grow *paka lōlō* ("crazy tobacco"), better known as marijuana, above Miloli'i's waterpipe intake on the south side of the stream. Apparently the shady conditions in the valley thwarted this horticultural endeavor, so when I stumbled across it all that remained as evidence were the planting bags scattered in the bush. I felt very lucky it was abandoned; protective *paka lōlō* growers make bushwhacking risky business in Hawai'i.

BEYOND MILOLI'I

South of Miloli'i lies Makaha Valley, which marks the southern end of Nā Pali Coast State Park. A 1-mile walk along the boulder beach from Miloli'i takes you to the mouth of this odd valley. The only entrance into the hanging valley floor follows the stream bed up over a series of small falls. Obviously this approach is passable only when the stream is dry, but even then it is dangerous in spots. The stream has cut a chasm 50 feet wide and 150 feet deep, with no wide valley floor to stroll up and a very real danger from falling rocks.

This seldom-visited valley is inhabited by a whole society of goats, which live on the rock ledges like ancient Indian cliff dwellers. We have also seen mule deer scrambling awkwardly over the boulder-strewn stream bed. Unlike the veteran goats, these deer are new-comers—they arrived from Oregon in the 1960s. In Hawai'i, only Kaua'i has these deer, locally referred to as black-tailed deer.

Atop the ridge that forms the south side of the valley, the navy runs a tracking station associated with the offshore submarine range and Pacific Missile Range Facility near Polihale. Travel beyond Miloli'i by boat requires clearance from the navy because they use these waters for training. When swimming or snorkeling you can hear a high-pitched beeping when the navy is tracking at sea.

Three miles of sheer cliff broken only by an occasional cleft form the remaining coastline. Finally, at Polihale Beach, the cliffs fade into the background and are replaced by a broad skirt of sand. Here the highway resumes at Polihale State Park. Fifteen miles of nature's finest handiwork separate this road from its other end at Kē'ē Beach.

INDEXED GLOSSARY

ahupua'a   A land division that sectioned each island   *33, 45*

air plant *(Bryophyllum pinnatum)*   An introduced succulent herb that seemingly lives on air   *30, 59*

'akoko *(Chamaesyce* spp.)   A family of plants that includes herbs, shrubs, and trees—all with a milky sap   *8*

Alapi'i   The point that separates Nu'alolo Kai and Nu'alolo 'Āina; literally means "ascent"   *4, 60, 61*

'a'o *(Puffinus newelli)*   The Newell's shearwater, a marine bird known also as Townsend's shearwater   *43, 73*

'ape *(Alocasia macrorrhiza)*   A relative of taro with immense, heart-shaped leaves   *33*

apple of Sodom *(Solanum hermanii)*   A poisonous plant that resembles the tomato, its relative; known in Hawaiian as *pōpolo kīkānia*   *37, 45*

'aumakua   A Hawaiian family's guardian spirit   *64*

'auwai   An irrigation ditch   *19, 34*

'awa *(Piper methysticum)*   An herb used to make a narcotic drink   *12*

Awa'awapuhi   A narrow, 3,000-foot-deep valley 7 miles west of Kē'ē Beach   *xx, 57–60*

'awapuhi *(Zingiber zerumbet)*   A wild ginger used by the Hawaiians for shampoo   *11, 37, 59*

be-still *(Thevetia peruviana)*   A poisonous, yellow oleander bush introduced from tropical America   *38, 45*

Big Pool   A swimming hole   *44, 46*

Brazilian cardinal *(Paroaria coronata)*   A gray bird with a red crest, also called the red-crested cardinal   *xxii, 3*

cardinal *(Cardinalis cardinalis)*   A red bird with a crest   *3*

castor bean *(Ricinus communis)*   A large, introduced weed with burlike fruit and poisonous seeds   *41*

Chinese thrush *(Garrulax canorus)*   An introduced songbird with green plumage and white eye markings   *40*

cocklebur *(Xanthium)*   A poisonous weed with burlike fruit   *41* coffee *(Coffea arabica)*   The cultivated Arabian coffee plant   *14, 19, 28, 30, 46, 53*

cone shell (Conidae)   A family of seashells notorious for having a poisonous sting   *71*

cowry shell (Cypraeidae)   Known to the Hawaiians as *leho*   *71*

dike   A vertical intrusion of rock formed when a lava flow cools and cracks then the cracks fill with fresh lava   *11, 20, 31, 46, 62*

endemic   Refers to plants and animals found only in one geographical location   *16, 20*

gecko (Gekkonidae)   An introduced lizard that changes the shade of its skin from off-white to charcoal brown   *xxii, 34*

ginger (Zingiberaceae)   A group of flowering forest herbs, often aromatic (see also *'awapuhi*)   *11, 18, 37, 59*

glottal stop (')   Marks a stopping sound in pronunciation like that between oh-oh   *xiv*

goat *(Capra hircus hircus)*   Often sighted on ridges along the coast   *xiv, xxi, 12, 13, 23, 30, 31, 35, 59, 74–75*

green flash   A small, momentary patch of emerald hue that occurs just as the sun sets   *xxii, 42, 72*

guava *(Psidium guajava)*   An introduced shrub with edible, seedy fruit   *xxi, 6, 18, 19, 37*

Hā'ena   The area near the end of Highway 560   *1, 39*

hala *(Pandanus odoratissimus)*   A native tree in the screwpine family with long leaves used for weaving   *xxi, 8, 13, 17, 49, 68*

hālau hula   A hula school, presided over by a hula master or *kumu hula*   *1, 4, 8, 9, 11, 25, 49*

hale   A Hawaiian dwelling or house   *14, 49, 68*

Hanakāpī'ai   The valley 2 miles in along the Kalalau Trail   *7, 13–19, 23, 49, 50*

Hanakoa   The valley with campsites 6 miles in on the Kalalau Trail   *7, 26–30, 52–53*

Hanalei   A town and large bay on Kaua'i's north shore   *xix, 55*

hanging valley   A valley with a floor that sits well above sea level   *23, 26, 52, 73*

haole   Originally a term for all foreigners, now largely used to refer to Caucasians   *xvii, xix, 6*

hau *(Hibiscus tiliaceus)*   A tangled tree that thrives along stream beds   *44, 45, 65*

Hawaiian monk seal *(Monachus schauinslandi)*   One of the two native Hawaiian land-based mammals   *71, 72*

he'e *(Polypus)*   The Hawaiian word for octopus   *64, 65, 71*

heiau   A Hawaiian place of worship   *1, 8, 38, 45, 49, 59, 66, 70*

hīhīwai *(Neritina granosa)* An edible, freshwater nerite that resembles the limpet *16, 74*

Hiʻiaka A younger sister of Pele *39*

hīnālea (Labridae) The family of wrasse fish that includes the ornate, Christmas, and saddle wrasses *65, 72*

hoary bats *(Lasiurus cinereus)* One of the two native mammals that inhabits the Hawaiian Islands *43*

Hōkūleʻa The Hawaiian name for the star Arcturus, which Polynesians used to navigate to Hawaii; literally means "clear star." Also the name of a double-hull canoe built in the 1970s to recreate Polynesian voyages *43*

Hono O Nā Pali A State Natural Area Reserve located between Hanakāpīʻai and Hanakoa valleys *21, 26*

Honopū The valley directly west of Kalalau *40, 56, 58*

honu (Cheloniidae) The Hawaiian term for all sea turtles, including the hawksbill and green sea turtles *60, 62, 65, 72*

Hoʻoleʻa A waterfall at Kalalau Beach; also called Kolea or Holea *38, 56*

Hoʻolulu The valley 4 miles in on the Kalalau Trail *21, 23–26, 50*

Hoʻolulu Sea Cave A cave noted for the waterfall across its entrance *50*

hoʻouluʻai Any agricultural *heiau* *45, 66, 67*

hukilau A fishing method where everyone on shore pulls *(huki)* two ends of a U-shaped leaf *(lau)* dragnet *41*

hula Hawaiian dances, originally done to chants without music *1, 4, 9, 11, 24, 25, 65, 67*

humpback whale *(Megaptera novaeangliae)* Hawaiʻi's state marine mammal *xxii, 50*

humuhumunukunukuāpuaʻa *(Rhinecanthus aculeatus)* A type of trigger fish; also the state fish of Hawaii *65*

humus Decayed plant material *31*

ʻieʻie *(Freycinetia arborea)* A native climbing screwpine *20, 24*

imu An underground oven that uses fire-heated rocks to cook food *11, 24*

indigenous Plants or animals that originated in and occur naturally throughout a region *xxi*

introduced Plants or animals brought to an area by man either intentionally or unintentionally *xxi, 10, 12, 16, 28, 45*

ironwood *(Casuarina equisetifolia)* An introduced tree that resembles a pine *4, 66, 70*

Java plum *(Syzygium cumini)* A naturalized tree with purple fruit *xxi, 4, 6, 37, 45, 74*

Ka'a'alahina   The eastern ridge at the mouth of Kalalau Valley   *35, 37, 55, 56*

kāhili   Standards made of bird feathers, symbolic of royalty   *23*

Kahuanui   An agricultural *heiau* in Kalalau Valley   *45*

kahuna   A member of a class of priests and highly skilled people   *17, 66*

kala *(Naso)*   The Hawaiian word for unicornfish   *65*

Kalāhū   The ridge above the Kalalau campsites; literally means "overflowing sun"   *45*

Kalalau   The largest valley along Nā Pali, and the end of the Kalalau Trail   *7, 33, 35–47, 55–58*

Kamaile   The peak above Nu'alolo Kai   *60, 62*

Kamapua'a   The pig demigod   *20, 43*

Kanaloa   The Hawaiian god of the wind and sea   *11, 67*

Kāne   The Hawaiian god that created all living things   *67*

kapu   A Hawaiian law—usually a restriction of religious nature; the meaning is the same as "tabu" and "taboo"   *11, 12, 44, 67, 68*

kauna'oa *(Cuscuta sandwichiana)*   A leafless, yellow, parasitic vine, also known as dodder   *30*

Keana Ma Waho   The large cave west of Ho'ole'a Falls at Kalalau Beach   *41*

Kē'ē Beach   The beach where Highway 560 ends and the Kalalau Trail begins   *xviii, xxii, 1, 4, 7, 17, 44, 47*

koa *(Acacia koa)*   A large forest tree fashioned into canoes by the Hawaiians   *28, 44*

koa'e *(Phaethon lepturus dorotheae)*   The white-tailed tropic bird   *23, 50*

koa haole *(Leucaena leucocephala)*   A feathery-looking, introduced weedy shrub   *41, 73*

koali 'awa *(Ipomea congesta)*   The Hawaiian term for the morning glory vine   *39, 41*

Kōke'e   The high mountain region behind Nā Pali   *8, 45, 59, 60, 74*

konohiki   A steward who managed an *ahupua'a* for one of Kaua'i's chiefs   *33, 68*

ko'oko'olau *(Bidens)*   A common trailside weed, some of which are native, while others, also called Spanish needle, are introduced   *xxi, 10*

Ko'olau   A Hawaiian who contracted leprosy and hid in Kalalau in the 1800s   *46, 55*

Kū   The Hawaiian god of war   *67*

kukui *(Aleurites moluccana)*   An early Polynesian introduction, now Hawai'i's state tree; also called the candlenut   *24, 35, 45, 68, 74*

Laka   The Hawaiian goddess of hula   *1, 4, 25*

lantana *(Lantana camara)*   A weedy relative of *oi*   *xxi, 34, 42, 59*

lau hala   The leaves of the *hala* tree   *8, 68*

lauhau *(Chaetodon unimaculatus* and *C. quadrimaculatus)*   A butterflyfish named for *hau* leaves   *65*

lauwiliwili *(Chaetodon miliaris)*   A butterflyfish that resembles the leaves of the *wiliwili* tree   *65*

lauwiliwili nukunuku ʻoiʻoi *(Forcipiger flavissimus* and *F. longirostris)*   A long-nosed fish that looks like *wiliwili* leaves   *65*

Lehua   A small island north of Niʻihau named for the *ʻōhiʻa lehua* flower   *9*

lei   A garland worn for adornment made from ferns, berries, leaf buds, seeds, or shells; now commonly made with flowers   *4, 9, 24, 25, 30, 37, 44*

lele koali   The Hawaiian verb to jump rope   *41*

limu   The general Hawaiian term for seaweed   *64–65*

Lohiʻau   A Kauaʻi chief; lover of Pele and Hiʻiaka   *1, 7, 39*

loli *(Holothuria)*   A large, black, sluglike sea cucumber   *64–65*

Lono   The god of harvest   *66–67*

lua   A hole or pit, now used to mean any type of toilet   *16, 28, 38, 70*

lūʻau   taro leaves; also the term for a feast   *19, 40*

macron (ˉ)   Indicates pronunciation of a long vowel   *xiv*

maiʻa *(Musa)*   The Hawaiian word for all types of bananas   *11*

maidenhair fern *(Adiantum)*   The common name for a group of native and introduced ferns   *20, 59, 73*

maile *(Alyxia olivaeformis)*   A vine that hula dancers used to adorn themselves and *hālau hula*   *25*

Makaha   The valley that forms the southern boundary of Nā Pali Coast State Park, 1 mile south of Miloliʻi   *75*

Makahiki   A four-month-long period of Hawaiian thanksgiving dedicated to Lono   *66–67*

makai   Indicates a seaward direction   *xii*

Makana Cliffs   The cliffs above Kēʻē Beach, and site for Hawaiian firefalls   *4, 47*

Makuaiki   A point at the western end of Nuʻalolo Kai   *68, 72*

mango *(Mangifera indica)*   A large tree bearing luscious fruit   *18, 44, 46*

Manono   A ridge at the western side of Hanakoa Valley, named for the Hawaiian term for the *Gouldia* plant   *29, 30, 35, 53*

manu ʻiwa *(Fregata minor palmerstoni)*   The Hawaiian name for the frigate bird, a seabird with wings that span 7 feet   *23*

mauka   Indicates an inland direction   *xii*

Menehune   A race of small people, perhaps mythical, said to have inhabited Kaua'i before the arrival of later Polynesians in A.D. 1250   *xviii, 14*

milo *(Thespesia populnea)*   A shade tree of early Polynesian introduction used for making cordage and wooden bowls   *41, 68*

Miloli'i ("fine twist")   A beach and valley 10 miles west of Kē'ē Beach   *xxii, 9, 68–75*

momi *(Columbella* and *Leptothyra)*   Miniscule shells used in making Ni'ihau shell leis   *71*

Mū   A tribe of supposedly mythical, banana-eating people similar to the Menehune   *xviii, 11, 58*

mule deer *(Odocoileus hemionus)*   In Hawaii also called black-tailed deer   *75*

myna *(Acridotheres tristis)*   A relatively large, dark brown bird introduced from India   *6*

Nākeikianā'i'iwi   A rock formation on the western edge of Kalalau Valley; literally meaning "the children of the *i'iwi* bird"   *45*

native   Plants or animals indigenous or endemic to a geographical region   *6, 10, 12, 14, 16, 21, 30, 42, 73–74*

naupaka *(Scaevola* spp.)   A group of native shrubs that includes different species found both by the shore and inland   *xxi, 17, 66*

Ni'ihau   An island 17 miles southwest of Kaua'i   *9, 10, 12, 35, 62*

noio *(Anous minutus melanogenys)*   A charcoal-colored marine bird, nicknamed "noddy"   *41, 50, 52*

noni *(Morinda citrifolia)*   A plant introduced by Polynesians with yellow fruit that smell like Camembert cheese when overripe   *42, 67*

Nu'alolo 'Āina   A valley east of Nu'alolo Kai   *xiv, 58, 59, 60, 68*

Nu'alolo Kai   Once the location of a fishing settlement, now a tour boat stop 8½ miles west of Kē'ē Beach   *xxii, 4, 35, 60–68*

'ōahi   Ancient Hawaiian firefall displays   *4, 47, 62*

ohana   The Hawaiian family unit   *xvii*

'ohe *(Bambusa vulgaris)*   The general Hawaiian term for bamboo   *18, 24*

'ōhi'a 'ai *(Eugenia malaccensis)*   A tree with pink, tufted flowers and edible, red fruit called mountain apple   *6, 25, 26*

'ōhi'a lehua *(Metrosiderous collina)*   An indigenous forest tree with red, tufted flowers   *6, 9, 26*

oi *(Stachytarpheta jamaicensis)*   The Hawaiian name for Jamaica vervain   *10*

ōkolehao   A liquor made from *ti* root   *45*

olonā *(Touchardia latifolia)*   An endemic plant with fibers stronger than those of the hemp plant   *33*

onionskin boulders Weathered boulders that peel away in layers *31, 45*

ʻoʻopu (Eleotridae and Gobidae) Native fish commonly found in Hawaiʻi's streams *15, 16, 70*

ʻōpae The Hawaiian term for shrimp *15, 16, 170*

Open-ceiling Cave A sea cave noted for its collapsed roof, located just east of Awaʻawapuhi Valley *58*

ʻopihi *(Cellana talcosa, C. sandwicensis,* and *C. melanostoma)* An edible limpet shaped like a Chinese hat *40, 58*

oxide A chemical in combination with oxygen *31*

Pacific Missile Firing Range A military base near Polihale *75*

paka lōlō *(Cannabis sativa)* The Hawaiian word for marijuana; literally translated as "crazy tobacco" *74*

pali The Hawaiian word for cliff; Nā pali means "the cliffs" *50, 70*

Pā Ma Waʻa The cove below Hoʻolulu Valley; literally meaning "the enclosure around canoes" *50*

papaya or pawpaw *(Carica papaya)* A tropical fruit tree *42*

passion fruit *(Passiflora)* Includes several species of introduced vines that bear ornate flowers, some with edible fruit (*P. seemannii* flowers hang like fragrant, purple chandeliers) *13, 38, 39*

Pele The Hawaiian volcano goddess *1, 9, 20, 39, 62*

piʻoi *(Dioscorea bulbifera)* A wild yam of early Polynesian introduction *19, 26*

Pōhakuao The *ahupuaʻa* between Hanakoa and Kalalau valleys *33–35, 53*

pōhinahina *(Vitex rotundifolia)* The Hawaiian name for beach vitex, a silvery, native beachside plant *42*

Polihale State Park A beach 15 miles southwest of Kēʻē Beach *75*

Polynesia The area bounded by New Zealand to the south, Easter Island to the east, and Hawaiʻi to the north *xxi, xvii, 11, 19, 43, 67*

pothos *(Pothos aureus, Scindapsus aureus)* An introduced tree-climbing vine, also common as a house plant *7*

Puanaiea The point west of Awaʻawapuhi Valley where a *heiau* is located; literally translated as "sickly or weak" *59*

puka The Hawaiian word for hole *35, 45*

pūpū A type of banana eaten after drinking bitter *ʻawa;* now refers to any type of appetizer *11, 12*

Puʻukula A knoll on Kaʻaʻalahina Ridge *35*

rainshadow The dry area located downwind of mountain ranges that induce rain *9*

red-tailed tropic bird *(Phaethon rubricauda rothschildi)* A seabird called *koaʻe ʻula* by the Hawaiians *23*

sennit   A rope twisted from fibers, often from coconut husk   *68*

shama thrush *(Copsychus malabaricus)*   A songbird from India   *40*

shield volcano   A type of volcano noted for its gentle slope; such volcanoes are typical in Hawai'i   *xviii*

sill   A dense horizonal layer of intrusive lava   *11, 20*

sisal *(Agave sisalana)*   A plant introduced for its potential as a fiber for rope making   *17, 18, 30, 34*

skink *(Scineidae)*   An introduced, shiny black lizard   *33, 34*

tannin   Tannic acid   *20*

tapa   Bark cloth, usually made from the paper mulberry tree *(wauke)*   *8, 24, 41, 42*

taro *(Colocasia esculenta)*   The staple root crop of the Hawaiians, introduced by Polynesian settlers   *14–15, 19, 34, 37, 45, 67, 71, 74*

ti *(Cordyline terminalis)*   A plant with long green leaves that sprout from a slender stalk   *11, 20, 23, 41, 45, 67*

tradewind   Hawai'i's prevailing northeast wind; the name is derived from the trading ships that depended on these winds   *xxii, 9, 29, 53*

tropical almond *(Terminalia catappa)*   An introduced tree with edible, almond-like seeds   *4*

tsunami   The word taken from Japanese for ocean waves associated with earthquakes, also (albeit improperly) referred to as tidal waves   *13*

uhi *(Dioscorea alata)*   A yam that grows in the wet regions of Kaua'i, originally brought by Polynesians   *26*

uhu *(Scarus perspicillatus)*   The Hawaiian name for the parrotfish   *64*

'ulili *(Heteroscelus incanus)*   A shorebird that winters in Hawai'i; known elsewhere as the "wandering tattler"   *16*

uluhe *(Dicranopteris linearis)*   The Hawaiian name for native false staghorn fern   *12, 73*

Waiahuakua   The valley 5 miles in on the Kalalau Trail   *21, 25, 26, 41, 52*

Waiahuakua Sea Cave   A sea cave noted for its two entrances and for the stream that gushes through its ceiling   *25, 52*

Wai Honu   A freshwater pool that forms on Kalalau Beach   *41*

Waimea   A town on the southwest coast of Kaua'i   *xix, 62*

wana *(Centrechinus paucispinus)*   The spiny sea urchin   *64, 65*

wedge-tailed shearwater *(Puffinus pacificus chlororhynchus)*   A marine bird that nests in burrows; called *'ua'u kani* by the Hawaiians   *43*

BIBLIOGRAPHY

Bennett, Wendell Clark. *Archaeology of Kauai.* Honolulu: Bernice P. Bishop Museum, 1931. Reprint. New York: Kraus Reprint Co., 1976.

Carlquist, Sherwin. *Hawaii: A Natural History.* Lawai, HI: Pacific Tropical Botanical Gardens, 1980.

Degener, Otto. *Plants of Hawaii National Parks Illustrative of Plants and Customs of the South Seas.* Ann Arbor: Braun-Brumfield, Inc., 1975.

Department of Geography, University of Hawaii. *Atlas of Hawaii.* Honolulu: University of Hawaii Press, 1983.

Dixon, George. *A Voyage Around the World: But More Particularly to the Northwest Coast of America.* London: George Goulding, 1789. Reprint. New York: Da Capo Press, 1968.

Elbert, S. H., (ed.). *Selections from Fornander's Hawaiian Antiquities and Folklore.* Honolulu: The University Press of Hawaii, 1979.

Emory, Kenneth P. "Ruins at Kee, Haena, Kauai." *Thrum's Hawaiian Annual.* Honolulu: Thrum, 1929.

Emory, Tiarre. "Hawaiian Life in Kalalau, Kauai, According to John Hanohano and His Mother Wahine-i-Keouli Pa." Bishop Museum Archives, Honolulu, 1949.

Gilman, G. D. "Journal of a Canoe Voyage along the Kauai Palis, Made in 1845." *Hawaii Historical Society Papers,* no. 14 (1908): 3–8.

Handy, E. S. Craighhill, and Elizabeth Green Handy. *Native Planters in Old Hawaii: Their Life, Lore, and Environment.* Honolulu: Bishop Museum Press, 1972.

Hinds, Norman E. A. *The Geology of Kauai and Niihau.* Honolulu: Bernice P. Bishop Museum, 1930. Reprint. New York: Kraus Reprint Co., 1971.

Hulme, Kathryn. *The Robert Allerton Story.* Kauai, HI: John Gregg Allerton, 1979.

Janion, Aubrey P. *The Olowalu Massacre and Other Hawaiian Tales.* Honolulu: Island Heritage Books, 1977.

Kimura, Bert, and Kenneth Nagata. *Hawaii's Vanishing Flora.* Honolulu: Oriental Publishing Co., 1980.

Knudsen, Eric A. "Some Personal Experiences on the Na Pali Coast." Paper presented at Kauai Historical Society, May 27, 1940, Kauai, Hawaii.

Krauss, Beatrice H. "Ethnobotany of Hawaii." Department of Botany, University of Hawaii, Honolulu, no date.

Lamoureux, Charles H. *Trailside Plants of Hawaii's National Parks.* Hawaii Volcanoes National Park: Hawaii Natural History Association, 1976.

Lewis, William J. *Interpreting For Park Visitors.* Philadelphia: Eastern Acorn Press, 1980.

Macdonald, Gordon A., Dan A. Davis, and Doak C. Cox. *Geology and Groundwater Resources of the Island of Kauai, Hawaii.* Honolulu: State of Hawaii, Division of Hydrography, 1960.

Neal, Marie C. *In Gardens of Hawaii.* Honolulu: Bishop Museum Press, 1965.

Pukui, Mary Kawena, and Samuel H. Elbert. *Hawaiian Dictionary* (revised edition). Honolulu: University of Hawaii Press, 1986.

Pukui, Mary Kawena, Samuel H. Elbert, and Esther T. Mookini. *Place Names of Hawaii* (revised edition). Honolulu: The University Press of Hawaii, 1974.

Randall, John E. *Underwater Guide to Hawaiian Reef Fishes.* Newtown, PA: Harrowood Books; co-published Kaneohe, HI: Treasures of Nature, 1981.

Rice, William Hyde. *Hawaiian Legends.* Honolulu: Bernice P. Bishop Museum, 1923. Reprint. New York: Kraus Reprint. Co., 1971.

Schmidt, Robert. "The Population of Northern Kauai in 1847." *Hawaii Historical Review* 2, no. 3 (1966): 303–304.

Shallenberger, Robert J., (ed.). *Hawaii's Birds.* Honolulu: Hawaii Audubon Society, 1978.

Stacey, Mary K. "Na Pali Coast Trip—Kauai, 1953." Bishop Museum, Honolulu. Photocopy.

Thrum, Thomas G. *Hawaiian Annual.* Honolulu: Thomas G. Thrum, 1889, 1899, 1900, 1905.

Thurston, Lorrin. "Exploring Nualolo, The Lost Hawaiian Kingdom." *Honolulu Advertiser* (July 16, 1922).

Titcomb, Margaret. *Native Use of Fish in Hawaii.* Honolulu: University Press of Hawaii, 1972.

Tomich, P. Quentin. *Mammals in Hawaii.* Honolulu: Bishop Museum Press, 1986.

Tomonari-Tuggle, Myra Jean F. *An Archaeological Reconnaissance Survey: Na Pali Coast State Park Island of Kaua'i.* Honolulu: State of Hawaii, Department of Land and Natural Resources, Division of State Parks, 1979.

ABOUT THE AUTHOR

Born in the Territory of Hawai'i in 1953, Kathy Valier was hiking into Nā Pali by the age of six. Her romance with the area bloomed seven years later while camping in remote Nu'alolo 'Āina Valley. Returning in 1975 from college in Colorado, she worked as a tour guide for ten years, four of them with Niele Tours, a company that she started with her husband, Norman.

In 1985 she received a master's degree in geography from the University of Hawai'i after completing a study of access in Nā Pali Coast State Park. She now lives in Kapaa, Kaua'i, from where she and Norman hike, bike, and kayak into Kaua'i's remote regions.

ADDRESS LIST

Division of State Parks
P.O. Box 1671
Lihue, HI 96766

3060 Eiwa Street
Lihue, Hawaii

(808) 245–4444

Hanalei Camping and Backpacking
P.O. Box 1245
Hanalei, HI 96714

(808) 826–6664

U.S. Navy (naval operations recorded message)
(808) 335–4229

Please send comments and questions to:

Kathy Valier
c/o University of Hawaii Press
2840 Kolowalu Street
Honolulu, HI 96822